THE
RESCUE

THE
RESCUE

SEVEN PEOPLE,
SEVEN AMAZING STORIES . . .

JIM CYMBALA

WITH ANN SPANGLER

BT INSPIRE

BROOKLYN, NEW YORK

BT Inspire

The Rescue

Copyright © 2017 The Brooklyn Tabernacle

Requests for information should be addressed to

The Brooklyn Tabernacle, 17 Smith Street, Brooklyn, NY 11201

Library of Congress Cataloging-in-Publication Data

Library of Congress Control Number: 2016963487

ISBN: 978-0-9978542-0-6

Cymbala, Jim, 1943-

All Scripture quotations, unless otherwise noted, are taken from *The Holy Bible, New International Version*®, NIV® Copyright © 1973, 1978, 1984, 2011 by Biblica, Inc.® Used by permission. All rights reserved worldwide.

Publishing project management by Lineage Media & Solutions, Inc.

First Printing

Printed in the United States of America

CONTENTS

—

Though the individuals whose stories are told in *The Rescue* are identified by name, a few people who appear in their stories have been given different names in order to protect their privacy.

THE RESCUE

Many of us feel hemmed in by impossible problems for which there are no easy solutions. Barraged by headlines that continually announce fresh trouble in the world, we feel deeply pessimistic, not just about what's going on in the world, but also about the state of our own lives and the lives of those we care about.

Perhaps we have achieved a measure of success but still feel empty inside, as though something is missing. No matter how much money we spend or how many relationships we have or how hard we work, struggle, play, or pretend, we can't find a sense of peace and happiness. A cloud still hangs over us.

Or maybe we are fighting personal battles—wrestling with financial challenges, struggling with addictions, facing a relationship breakup, suffering from sickness, or battling the effects of abuse.

As I travel throughout the country, I often meet people so battered by life that their hope seems as fragile as a candle burning in a rainstorm. One more gust of wind—one more difficulty or challenge—and the flickering flame will be snuffed out, leaving them in total darkness. If they are not discouraged about their own lives, they are deeply concerned by what's happening in the lives of their children or others they care about.

Fortunately, we don't have to live like that, feeling beaten down by life's challenges or hopeless about the future. No matter how strong our personal storm or how difficult our life circumstances may be, we can emerge with strength and hope.

—

No matter how strong our personal storm or how difficult our life circumstances may be, we can emerge with strength and hope.

—

Instead of feeling confused, defeated, angry, and depressed, we can begin to experience life in a way that will bring profound healing and deep peace. We will not need to keep repeating self-destructive behaviors or be victimized by forces we can't control. Instead we will be able to face the future with hope and expectation.

How can we do this? Is there a seven-step plan or a secret path to success that will yield these benefits? Is there a how-to book that will magically solve our worst problems? You probably know there is not.

Rather than offering you a spirited pep talk, or a set of persuasive arguments, or a self-help manual that promises to improve your life, I simply want to share a few remarkable stories. Though each of these stories is unique and dramatic, all of them revolve around common problems and struggles, some of which you may have experienced at one time or another in your own life. Or perhaps someone close to you has.

If I had a big enough house, I'd invite you into my living room to sit down with me and the seven friends whose stories I tell. As you listened to each of them, a window would open up, offering you a glimpse not only into their pain and confusion but also into the joy and peace they've found as a result of a profound transformation. In that intimate setting, you would be able to watch the expressions on their faces and hear the tone of their voices as they recounted their experience of being rescued from impossible situations.

But since my wife and I live in a small one-bedroom apartment in downtown Brooklyn, that's not possible. Instead I've done my best to share these stories in the way they were told to me. As you pick up this small book, I hope the miles between us will shrink until you feel as though we are all sitting down together and that you are listening to each of my friends as they speak openly and honestly about what has happened to them.

But why these particular stories and not others? Truthfully, I could have found countless stories that are every bit as gripping. Such stories happen every day across our country and around the world. I've chosen these because I know the people personally and because I believe that the stories of their transformation have the potential to transform your life and the lives of those you care about. To my seven friends whose stories are told in this book—to Lawrence, Timiney, Rich, Robin, Kaitlin, Alex, and Toni—I say thank you for your honesty and courage. I am profoundly grateful for your willingness to tell the truth so that others can be helped. Thank you for giving me the privilege of sharing your stories.

To everyone else, my hope is that, like my seven friends, you will experience the deep transformation that I call "the rescue"—an experience that will change your life so that you will no longer feel defeated by your problems or overwhelmed by your worries. Instead you will have learned what it means to live a life of profound transformation, one that will bring you joy and give you the kind of peace that will never leave you.

LAWRENCE'S STORY

———

LAWRENCE PUNTER IS A FORMER COLLEGE ATHLETE AND
FLIGHT INSTRUCTOR. A SUCCESSFUL ENTREPRENEUR AND
BUSINESSMAN, HE IS ALSO A MEMBER OF THE GRAMMY
AWARD-WINNING BROOKLYN TABERNACLE CHOIR. IF
YOU MET HIM——ALL SIX FEET FIVE INCHES OF HIM——YOU
WOULD NEVER GUESS THAT THIS HANDSOME, SOFT-SPOKEN
MAN, WHO OFTEN SHARES HIS STORY IN PRISONS, WAS ONCE
A BOY NOBODY SEEMED TO LOVE.

I ROLL OVER IN BED, bone tired. I've been lying here for most of a day, grateful at least for clear skies and bearable temperatures. Even when sunlight breaks through the clouds and makes me squint through my closed eyelids, I force myself back to sleep, since dreams are my only relief.

—

Dreams are my only relief.

—

My makeshift bedroom is not located in a cozy apartment or a comfortable home. It's not tucked away in a friend's guest-house or out on a screened-in porch. Night after night I sleep in a place without windows or walls, on a dingy mattress in a dirty alleyway between two apartment buildings.

Except when someone wanders through to toss a bag of trash in the dumpster, I am by myself. There is the occasional rat, as well as buzzing flies during the day and swarms of mosquitoes at night. I wonder if I'll go deaf slapping my ears to shoo them away so I can get some rest. I've been living like this for months—light-headed, dizzy, and alone.

Tonight I feel a sense of relief, as though something might go right for a change. Soon there will be no more pain or struggling, no more hunger and fighting battles I cannot win. I hold the pills in one hand and a water bottle in the other. In a little while it will all be over. I am going to sleep forever. I will never have to wake up again.

————

What kind of path does a young guy take to arrive at a place like this? In my case the journey began before I was born.

I don't know how my parents met or what attracted them to each other. It doesn't matter. What does matter is that when they were still very young they married. I know nothing about how my dad reacted when he heard the news that he was going to be a father. Maybe he tried to smile. Maybe my mom pretended to be happy. I only know that he walked out on her when she was nine months pregnant.

Whether it was one woman or a string of women, I'm not certain. But he'd already had several affairs during the course of their short marriage. By the time my mother gave birth to me at a hospital in New York, there was no loving husband out in the waiting room. Nor was there a proud dad to take me in his arms and welcome me into the world.

So my parents divorced, and for a short time it was just my mom and me. Single moms are not uncommon, of course. Most of them struggle and work hard and love their children no matter what. But my mother was not like them. She wasn't a hidden hero who everyone would someday praise for all her sacrifices. To her I was just an inconvenience. Like my father, she wanted a new beginning, and a baby would only hold her back.

When I was two or three months old, my mom dropped me off in Antigua, an island in the West Indies, where my grandmother lived. Then she returned to New York.

For the first few years, I was happy. I was a child like every other child. It didn't bother me that my "mom" was so much

older than other kids' mothers. I never noticed. I just knew that she took care of me and that I loved her. She may have told me I had another mother who lived in a strange place called New York City. But if she did, it never registered.

Unwanted by my mother and father, I spent the first seven years of my life in Antigua.

By the time I was seven, my grandmother decided that things needed to change. It wasn't right for a mother to be separated from her son. Plus her daughter was old enough now to take care of her child. So just like that, I was separated from everyone and everything I loved and packed off to New York to live with a reluctant stranger who happened to be my mother.

The abuse began gradually. Because I looked so much like my father, I was a constant reminder to my mother of all the terrible things he had done to her.

I would spill milk, and she would hit me. I would say something wrong, words that another mother might verbally correct. She would hit me again. Pretty soon she was lashing me with belts and hitting me with her shoes. Once she broke the heel off a favorite pair while hitting me over the head.

After a while she moved up to extension cords, twisting them into whips and thrashing me with the plug end, covering my body with welts.

We had relatives in the city who knew about the abuse because she never tried to hide it, even at family gatherings. "Stop it—you're going to kill him!" my aunts would yell. But she never stopped and they never reported it. Because of the constant abuse, I became very introverted, extremely shy and quiet.

I got picked on at school too. The kids bullied me because I spoke with a West Indian accent. I was different enough to stand out. In Antigua I'd had friends and someone to love me. But in New York I had no one.

—

In Antigua I'd had friends and someone to love me. But in New York I had no one.

—

When I was in middle school, gangs were everywhere. Today you might hear about the Crips and the Bloods or even the Stack Money Goons or the Very Crispy Gangsters. Back then it was the Tomahawks, the Black Spades, and the Jolly Stompers. If you're a sports fan, you might know that Mike Tyson became a member of the Jolly Stompers when he was eleven years old.

One day twenty to thirty guys surrounded me while I walked home from school. "You're drafted into the Jolly Stompers," they said, as though it was already a done deal. "Show up at the courtyard tonight at 11:00." But I was a naïve kid from the West Indies who wanted nothing to do with gangs, and I ignored them.

When they caught up with me the next day, they held me down and started punching and kicking me. "Be at the meeting tonight at 11:00," they told me. I thought about letting my mother know what was happening, but I was afraid she would get angry and beat me up herself. Fearful and not knowing what to do, I stayed home again.

The next day when they found me, they pushed me down and began stomping on me. "We know where you live and what bus your mother takes to work. If you don't show up tonight, something bad is going to happen to her." Even though I thought my mother hated me, I didn't want them to hurt her.

—

Even though I thought my mother hated me, I didn't want them to hurt her.

—

Since she worked the night shift as a nurse at a local hospital, it was easy for me to leave the house without her knowing. After she went to work, I made my way to the courtyard. That night I learned how new members join a gang. You enter into one-on-one combat with the leader. In my case that was a joke.

How could a thirteen-year-old stand up against a twenty-year-old? I knew I was about to be slaughtered.

I remember how it began—with a fist to my chin. My opponent pummeled me so hard and fast that I didn't get a punch in. After kneeing me in the gut, he hammered my bent-over back with his fists until I collapsed. After kicking and stomping on me, he let the other guys pile on. Finally when he decided I'd had enough, the beating abruptly stopped.

Lying on the ground, looking up at the guys who had so viciously attacked me, I remember thinking how strange it was to see them smiling down at me. Then everyone burst into laughter.

Pulling me to my feet, the leader hugged me and said, "Now you're one of us. We're your family. Anyone messes with you, they mess with us." Then forty or fifty guys took turns hugging and congratulating me.

Instead of feeling hurt or enraged, I felt happy about what had happened—almost elated. Finally somebody wanted me to be part of their group. I was so glad to belong. After congratulating me, the leader handed me the uniform of a Jolly

Stomper—a jean jacket with cut-out sleeves and the gang's insignia painted on the back.

Everyone had a nickname, something like "Fat Boy," "Slinky," or "Ghost." It was a way of reinforcing our gang identity. Since I was tall for my age, they called me "Shorty."

When I showed up at school the next day in a Jolly Stomper uniform, no one hassled me. The bullies who had made my life miserable turned into instant cowards, terrified of what the gang might do to them if they caused me any more trouble.

Wow! I was beginning to enjoy the benefits of being part of a gang. I belonged to those guys and they belonged to me. But belonging brought obligations. I had a job to do.

At that time there were about 120 members of the Jolly Stompers. Our specialty was robbing small stores and holding people up on the street. Most of the guys were eighteen, nineteen, or twenty. As the youngest member, I was like a mascot. "Shorty," they would say, "tonight we're gonna rob a bodega" (a small grocery store). "We don't want you to get hurt, so just stay outside and be the lookout. If anybody comes while we're inside, just yell."

I remember one small market that we robbed repeatedly. It was a mom-and-pop store run by an elderly couple. Over and over those two old people would huddle in the corner watching as the gang ransacked their place, grabbing beer from the fridge and money from the cash drawer. When they were finished, I would come in to collect my share, stuffing my pockets full of candy and bubble gum.

I can still picture the people we victimized, especially that old couple. I felt horrible about what we were doing but didn't know how to stop.

—

I felt horrible about what we were doing but didn't know how to stop.

—

Even though I was running with a gang, I was still a quiet, introverted kid at home. "You're just like your father!" my mother would scream. "You're useless; good for nothing!" Though she kept on beating me, I never tried to defend myself, because I thought that was how parents treated their kids. What my mother didn't know was that at night while she was working, I was out roaming the streets. I was also skipping school, hanging out and drinking beer with other guys in the gang.

Being a Jolly Stomper meant not only that you were part of a family but also that you had common enemies. Street wars could erupt quickly if another gang thought you were invading their turf, or if someone felt disrespected, or if there was an argument over a girl. At that time it was mostly knives, bats, brass knuckles, and chains, but there were guns too.

One day word went out that we were to show up at midnight fully armed for a rumble with the Tomahawks. As soon as the fighting began, it was clear who was going to win, because we were vastly outnumbered. Every Jolly Stomper escaped but me. I had counted on fellow gang members to have my back, but that was a fantasy. They were just too scared.

Before I knew it I was down on the concrete with twenty guys piling on. They took turns kicking me and stomping on my head. One of them stabbed me with a metal spike.

This is it, I thought. *I'm thirteen years old and I am going to die. They're going to kick me to pieces—break my arms, legs, ribs, everything!* I absorbed blow after blow until I grew numb to the pain. Curled into a ball with my arms wrapped around my head, I knew I would be dead if they didn't stop soon. I felt myself slipping into unconsciousness.

But then, out of the blue, I heard sirens. When the cops arrived, everybody scattered. I don't know what tipped them off. Maybe they were cruising the neighborhood. But the area we were fighting in wasn't visible from the street. Plenty of times they didn't find out about fights until they were over, if they even found out at all. But that night they showed up just in time to save my life.

The Tomahawks had done a number on me. My face was so swollen I couldn't open my eyes, but at least I was alive. Instead of going home and facing my mother's wrath, I stayed at my aunt's house until I got better.

She convinced my mother that if we stayed in Brooklyn I would end up either dead or in jail. So overnight we moved to Miami. I couldn't believe the difference. Compared to New York, it looked like paradise, filled with green lawns and nice homes.

Instead of running with gangs, I started getting involved in sports. "Which team are you going to join?" everyone kept asking. When the basketball coach saw how tall I was, he said,

"We want you for the team." When the football coach saw me, he said, "No, you're coming out for football."

Things were getting better at home too. By the time I was sixteen, my mother started giving me more space. The beatings were less frequent even though she kept calling me a no-good juvenile delinquent who was just taking up space on the planet. I heard it so often that I thought she must be right.

Fortunately I was good at basketball—very good. I'd started playing the game in middle school. By my senior year I was an MVP and an All-American. With that came five college scholarships. Normally if you're in high school and you make MVP and All-American, your parents are excited. *Wow, Mom, do you believe it? Dad, I made All-American! Look I was offered five scholarships! Which one should I take?*

But my dad wasn't around, and my mom didn't care. She hadn't planned to send me to college anyway. So my coach helped me decide which scholarship to accept. Auburn offered me free tuition but with no room and board, so I chose a small college in Atlanta that covered all my expenses.

At first things went well in class and on the basketball court. I began to feel better about myself and more hopeful about the future. Maybe my mother was wrong about me. Maybe I could make something of my life. But during my sophomore year, I suffered a severe leg injury that ended my basketball career. Without a scholarship, I had to drop out. I returned home in a full leg cast that reached to my thigh.

But home was different now. My mother had a new husband and a baby, and I didn't fit in. She wanted nothing to do with a good-for-nothing son who reminded her of her rotten ex-husband.

As soon as my cast came off, I returned to New York and found a summer job. My dream had always been to attend flight school. Since I was six feet five, an inch too tall for the Air Force, I picked out a school in Tulsa, Oklahoma, that was advertised in the newspaper. Between the money I earned from the job and a gift from my aunt and uncle, I had $1,000 in my pocket when I boarded a bus to Tulsa.

After enrolling in school, I quickly found a roommate and a dishwashing job at Denny's. Here was another chance to make good. *So what if I don't have parents*, I thought. *I made MVP and All-American by myself. I'm doing great on my own.* And I was.

But after a while I lost my job at Denny's. My boss assured me I would be hired back as soon as business picked up. It shouldn't be long. Fortunately my roommate was willing to carry me until I returned to work. But Denny's never called back, and I couldn't find another job. After several weeks my roommate reluctantly asked me to leave. He needed someone who could help him make the rent.

—

I was determined to make it on my own, to show my relatives that I could amount to something.

—

Because it seemed like a temporary setback, I wasn't about to run back to New York. I was determined to make it on my own, to show my relatives—especially the ones who hadn't intervened to stop my mother's abuse—that I could amount to something.

For a while I depended on friends from Denny's who took turns letting me sleep on their couches. I kept promising to get myself together. But I was spiraling downward. When I finally ran out of friends to stay with, I landed out on the street.

Most people think of addiction or mental illness when they think about the homeless. But as an athlete, I had always carefully avoided drugs and alcohol, even when everyone else was snorting coke and popping pills. But I was depressed, so down that it must have been hard to be around me.

With nowhere to go, I settled into the alley behind my old apartment building. One day I noticed a family who was moving out of their apartment. They threw a bunch of stuff into the dumpster, including an old mattress. As soon as they left, I dragged it out and brushed it off. From then on I slept on that dingy mattress in a dirty alleyway between two apartment buildings.

One of my friends from Denny's was still trying to help me out. He would put leftovers in a plastic bag and then deposit it in the dumpster where I would find it. But after a while he stopped doing that. Desperate for money, I began selling my plasma to the local blood bank twice a week. Each donation netted me $7, most of which went for loaves of bread to fill me up.

Why didn't I get help or go to a homeless shelter? I thought those were for old people or down-and-outers. I was an

All-American, a guy studying to be a pilot. I was going to find my own way out of my troubles.

When you live on the streets, you can't get clean. You never feel safe, and you have no privacy. There's no shelter from bad weather, and there is never enough to eat. I remember lying in that alleyway and wondering how I had sunk so low. How did I get here? There was no other answer than the one my mother had always given me: I was worthless, no good, a big zero just like my father. I was a piece of garbage living next to a garbage can. All her predictions about me had come true.

—

**All my mother's predictions
about me had come true.**

—

Sleep became the way I escaped. When I slept, I stopped feeling hungry and lonely.

I remember having a vivid dream about the old movie *The Sound of Music*. Instead of merely watching it, I become part of it, running and twirling around with Julie Andrews in that green meadow. As long as I am dreaming, I am happy. But then I wake up and see that I am still dirty, hopeless, and hungry.

I'm lightheaded, dizzy, and alone. By now I have sold so much plasma that the nurse has trouble finding a vein to extract my blood.

Finally I make a decision. *You know what,* I say to myself. *I love to sleep so much that I am going to go to sleep and keep on sleeping. I am not going to wake up anymore. I'm tired of living like this. My father doesn't care about me. My mother doesn't care about me. Nobody cares about me. I can't live like this anymore. I've had enough.*

Instead of buying bread with the money I earn selling my blood, I decide to purchase a bottle of sleeping pills. I am going to go to sleep, and I am going to stay in that meadow forever, twirling around in the sunshine with the mountains all around me.

Since my bed is sandwiched between two apartment buildings, I am used to hearing radios and televisions blaring from open windows. Tonight as I sit on that mattress, grasping the pills in one hand and a water bottle in the other, I suddenly hear the sound of a man's voice. It is coming from a nearby apartment.

The voice is crystal clear, and I can tell it belongs to a preacher. "God loves you," he says. "Jesus Christ gave his life for you." There is so much kindness in that voice, so much tenderness, that I begin to cry uncontrollably. He seems to be talking just to me. "He died to give you a new beginning." His words slip into that dark place in my heart where there is no hope. I feel something lifting, something changing inside me. I keep listening.

—

His words slip into that dark place in my heart where there is no hope. I feel something lifting, something changing inside me.

—

It would be wrong to say I am surprised by what I hear. No, I am shocked. *There really is a God, and he loves me!* Now the man says I should invite Jesus into my heart. I look up into the night sky, up to heaven, and say, "I accept you; I accept you; I accept you into my life. I don't know what it means, but I accept you." I beg Jesus to come in, and he does, bringing so much peace. It washes over me, and I am surrounded by it.

The next morning shafts of sunlight wake me. I am still lying on that dingy mattress in that dirty alleyway, but everything has changed. I feel different, like something inside has shifted. *He's got me,* I think. *I'm going to be okay.*

―――――

Looking back on that time, I am amazed at how much joy a person can feel in the midst of such terrible circumstances.

Later that day I headed over to Denny's to see if my friend could give me something to eat. "Listen," he said, "the manager's looking for a dishwasher for one night a week. Maybe I can talk to him and get you hired again." Then he invited me to his apartment so I could clean up and apply for the job.

It was minimum wage and only one night a week, but I was hired. Before long, one night turned into three nights, which turned into a full-time job. To supplement this income, I started working at a motel across the street from Denny's. From 7 a.m. to 3 p.m. I was a handyman, fixing beds and chairs at the motel, and from 11 p.m. to 7 a.m., I was a dishwasher at Denny's. Pretty soon I had enough money to abandon the alleyway, rent a room, and return to flight school.

It wasn't long before I received my pilot's license. I'll never forget my first solo flight. I had done it! It didn't matter that my parents hadn't helped me, because God had helped me. All those terrible things my mother had said about me were just a great big lie—a lie that no longer controlled me or my future.

After completing flight school I returned to New York. I got every kind of license you can get, one by one—a commercial pilot's license, a flight instructor's license, and an instrument flight instructor's license. That meant I was qualified to teach pilots how to become flight instructors.

When my uncle took note of how well I was doing, he got me a job with a union contractor that paid far better than what a flight instructor could ever make. So I worked a construction job in Manhattan during the week and as a flight instructor on the weekends. After a while I started two different companies—a home improvement company and an air taxi. By then I was doing so well that I had no worries about having enough.

Several years after experiencing Christ's love in that alleyway in Tulsa, I began slipping away from God. Even though I knew Jesus had rescued me, I hadn't really grown in my faith. Now that I was financially secure, I began drifting away, thinking I could handle things on my own.

When I was twenty-one I got married, but I had no idea how to be a good husband. My wife and I had so many problems that our marriage collapsed in less than two years. After that I lived with a girlfriend and we had a child together. Within a year, that relationship failed too.

One day someone invited me to a choir concert at Madison Square Garden. We were going to meet outside but she never showed up. It was a Friday night and I had nothing to do, so instead of heading home, I decided to go in for a few minutes. I thought I would listen to a little music and then leave. Plus I was curious. How could a church choir manage to fill up New York's premier concert venue?

But the music was so beautiful and the stories people told about how God had changed their lives were so powerful that I could have stayed all night.

Then a man began speaking. I don't remember everything he said that night, but he spoke about God's love in a way that pierced my heart. It felt as though God himself was sitting right next to me, putting his arm around me and telling me things. *All these years you've been looking for a father, someone to watch over and protect you. But you have a father, and your father is right here with you. I will give you the love you've been yearning for. I will help you fight your battles and live your life.*

—

I will give you the love you've been yearning for. I will help you fight your battles and live your life.

—

In that moment I completely surrendered my life to Christ. I understood that he was the bridge to my heavenly Father.

"My father, my dad, my daddy, my God," I began to say. Here I was, this former gang-banger, juvenile delinquent, and athlete, and this is how I was talking to God because he had become the love of my life.

After that I started attending the church that sponsored the concert. As I prayed and as others prayed with me, God started healing me. All the scars from everything that had happened to me began to fade away. I had felt so empty inside, but now the void was filled. It didn't matter anymore that my parents had never told me they loved me and that they probably never would. I had all the love I needed. My healing depended on God, not on them.

Sometimes when I picture Jesus, I see him with the nail prints still in his hands. That makes me think of my own wounds. Because he rose from the dead, Jesus' wounds point to his victory. Because I belong to him, my wounds do too.

After a while I met a woman who attended the same church. Instead of being excited about the relationship, I was frightened by my feelings. I had already concluded that I would never make a good father or husband because of my family background. Weren't my other attempts at intimacy proof enough of that?

"Whenever you see me," I told her, "please avoid me. Just go the other way." For the next six months we kept out of each other's way. If she saw me in the lobby or in the balcony of the church, she would turn around and walk in the opposite direction. And I would do the same.

During that time I told God, *I love you more than life itself, but I will never get married because my relationships in the past have all ended in shambles.* One day while I was praying, I thought I heard him saying to me, *You're about to lose the best thing that will ever happen to you.* It seemed as though he was speaking to me as my Father, promising to teach me everything I needed to learn so that I wouldn't lose the woman I loved.

Not long after that I managed to catch her attention, even though she was trying to avoid me. Though we hadn't spoken to each other in six months, the words came spilling out of my mouth: "I don't know how to be a good husband or a good dad. But I love you, and I don't think God wants me to let you go. Will you give me one more chance?"

I was so awkward and ineloquent, and I had no idea what she was thinking. Without looking at me or saying a word, she turned and walked away. I felt like such a fool.

An hour later she called to say that she loved me too. A few months later we were married. Despite my past, God blessed me with a remarkable woman. After eight years of marriage, I can look back at all the love she's poured into

Celebrating a moment I never thought would happen

me and see how God has worked through her to bring more healing into my life.

Two months ago, we had a baby girl and named her Grace. Little Gracie reminds the two of us of all the blessings God has showered on us even though we know we don't deserve them.

There's a song called "God Is Singing over Me." I know that God has indeed sung over me. He has seen my suffering and heard my cries. At the right time, he said, "Enough!" Enough pain, enough darkness, enough of not knowing him. The time for my release had come.

Since that night in the alleyway, I've asked myself many times, *Why was the TV tuned to that particular program? Why did the preacher start talking about Christ's love just as I was about to swallow those pills? What if the people who lived there had gone out that night? What if they hadn't opened their windows?* I'd been squatting in that alleyway for months. But in all that time I had never heard anyone talking about God or his love. Why did everything line up so perfectly that night?

Because God knew. He knew when the timing was right, the exact moment when my heart would be open to him.

The truth is that he knows the right moment in everybody's life.

He doesn't ignore our cries for help. If we entrust ourselves to him, he will unwind and untwist every lie the enemy has ever told us. He will heal us and make us whole.

—

If we entrust ourselves to him, he will unwind and untwist every lie the enemy has ever told us.

—

Sometimes people draw near to God and then slip back, like I did. Their affection for him cools off. Even then he keeps pursuing us. Keeps running after us. Surely he is who he says he is—the Father of the fatherless, the one who is ready to put his arms around us and claim us as his own.

TIMINEY'S AND RICH'S STORIES

———

TIMINEY VISSER GREW UP IN AUSTIN, TEXAS. HER BRIGHT PERSONALITY AND WELCOMING SMILE MAKE YOU THINK OF A CHEERLEADER OR A FLIGHT ATTENDANT, A NATURAL OPTIMIST AND EXTROVERT. FOR SEVERAL YEARS SHE WORKED FOR AN INTERNATIONAL AIRLINE THAT TOOK HER TO SOME OF THE WORLD'S MOST GLAMOROUS DESTINATIONS. MEETING HER, YOU WOULD NEVER GUESS THAT SHE HAD A PAST SHE COULD NOT OUTRUN.

RICH CRISALLI IS A FORMER WALL STREET TRADER. A PARTNER IN A SUCCESSFUL FIRM, HE HAD EVERYTHING HE WANTED: EXPENSIVE CARS, A MILLION DOLLAR HOME, AND PLENTY OF GIRLFRIENDS. WHY WAS HE SO UNHAPPY?

TIMINEY

—

CHURCH WAS ALWAYS part of my life, the memory of it as vivid as my recollections of home. But unlike the light-drenched skies above Austin, Texas, where I grew up, my memories of church are tinged with darkness.

My earliest memories of my father are dark too. When you're five years old and about to travel to British Columbia to meet your dad for the first time, and when people anoint you with oil and pray over you, asking God to protect you as though your father is the devil incarnate, it has a way of casting shadows across the past.

It wasn't that my dad was a bad guy. The problem was that he was an outsider. He didn't belong to the church.

—

**We belonged to a church that
controlled every aspect of our lives.**

—

I grew up knowing my mother loved God and that he had acted powerfully in her life after she and my father divorced when I was a toddler. But it took me a while to realize that we belonged to a church that controlled every aspect of our lives.

My first visit with my dad must have gone well because I spent every summer after that with him and his new family. I loved those Canadian summers, because I felt free to be like the other kids, wearing shorts, watching television, swimming, water-skiing, and having fun.

It must have puzzled my father when I showed up every year with only skirts and dresses stuffed into my suitcase. Each summer he and my stepmom would take me shopping for shorts and a swimsuit. Though he may have known I wasn't allowed such liberties at home, I never talked to him about all the rules.

The longer I attended church, the better I got at hiding the truth about how I felt. As I grew older, it was just too painful to explain to classmates that I couldn't play sports or march in the school band because doing so would mean wearing a uniform with pants. So I shrugged it off, pretending I liked wearing ankle-length skirts and didn't enjoy wearing flip-flops, even when the Texas heat soared past one hundred degrees. That seemed far better than telling the truth: that I wasn't allowed to expose my legs or toes because that would be immodest.

Like anyone else at that age, I didn't want to stick out. I wanted to blend in with the other girls, to be able to paint my toenails or look in the mirror and see myself with a little jewelry and makeup. But that, too, was forbidden.

There were other restrictions as well. Afraid that young people might fall into sexual sin, the church encouraged early marriages. Anyone who stumbled in this area was shunned, because the church taught that because Jesus died only once, nobody got more than one chance at forgiveness unless the pastor and elders decided otherwise. Once you belonged to the church, you were supposed to be perfect.

Many girls were married when they were fourteen. Fortunately my dad heard about the practice and intervened to make sure that wouldn't happen to me.

Even adults were subject to church control. In some instances, you couldn't apply for a new job or head out of town on a trip without asking the pastor's permission. There was also a lot of pressure to cut off ties with family members and friends who didn't belong to the church.

Though I loved my summers of freedom, I felt conflicted and confused as I shuttled back and forth between Texas and Canada. I was worried I might spend eternity in hell for wearing bathing suits and watching movies; I was certain that God was angry and disappointed with me.

—

I was worried I might spend eternity in hell for wearing bathing suits and watching movies.

—

Afraid to voice my confusion because that would have been seen as rebellion, as "bucking the Holy Spirit," I wondered privately where in the Bible it said you couldn't have dreams, couldn't explore your talents by playing sports, marching in the band, or becoming a cheerleader.

At least I was allowed to go to the junior-senior prom—but that was only because I was class president. Even then I had to show the pastor a picture of my date, assuring him we were only friends.

I struggled for years until I decided that I had no choice but to part ways with the church. As much as I had yearned for freedom, leaving was painful, like ripping a bandage off a festering wound that might never heal. Because I'd grown up in that church, its members were like aunts and uncles and brothers and sisters to me. So when I left, it was like divorcing my extended family.

My memories of church were tinged with darkness.

After that no one spoke to me. They were simply following the rules, because now I was on the outside.

After moving out of the house, I lived with a girlfriend. For the first time in my life, at the age of twenty-four, I was beginning to learn to think for myself and make decisions on my own. I started by taking a course to become a certified paralegal. When I began to date, I got my heart broken a couple of times because I was so naïve.

Though I wanted to live a moral life, I was determined to have nothing to do with religion. Because of how I had grown up, faith seemed like a joke, like something surreal. The God I learned about didn't do anything for me but get me hurt and broken. Why would I want to believe in him? Why would

I want to follow him? Attending a wedding or funeral at a church would be enough to set off alarm bells. Simply being inside a church and hearing the Bible read would make my stomach churn.

Underneath everything was an impermeable layer of fear. Struggling with suicidal thoughts, I began meeting with a therapist, hoping she could help me untangle the hurts of my past.

One day while I was making online travel arrangements for my boss, I saw a help-wanted ad from a major commercial airline. All those summers shuttling back and forth from Texas to British Columbia had made me dream of becoming a flight attendant. On a whim I sent in an application. After a series of interviews, I was offered a job and given two weeks to decide.

Two weeks to take the leap—or not. Two weeks to find out if I had the guts to say yes to my lifelong dream. Accepting the job would mean leaving my Texas bubble behind and moving to New Jersey, where I would be based. I'd be thrust into a completely different culture where I wouldn't know anyone. Somehow I found the nerve to say yes.

Working as a flight attendant was absolutely awesome. After living such a small life in Texas, suddenly I was living big, jetting off to London, Paris, and Geneva. Like the proverbial bird in a cage, I had spread my wings and flown away.

—

**As proud as I was of forging a
new life for myself, I was still
fighting the ghosts of my past.**

—

As proud as I was of forging a new life for myself, I was still fighting the ghosts of my past. Now that I was further from the church in both time and distance, feelings I had tried to block began to assert themselves. It was like someone had twisted the knob of a stove all the way to high. Simmering emotions began boiling up, and I had to deal with them. But I didn't know how. I felt angry and resentful. *Why had I felt so ashamed whenever I broke the slightest rule? Why had I been forced to hide my thoughts and deny my feelings? I'd never been allowed to explore my talents or even learn from my own mistakes. Why had I been deprived of a normal childhood?*

Even while I was having these interior struggles, flying continued to bring me joy. I liked meeting new people and exploring different cultures whenever time allowed.

One morning, I was working a flight with a layover in Miami. As I checked the seats to make sure tray tables were up and baggage stowed, I had no idea that I had boarded a flight that was about to take me into uncharted territory.

Responding to a call button as we were readying the plane for departure, I saw a guy sitting by himself. He looked a bit rough, like he hadn't shaved or showered. I wondered if he might be nursing a hangover.

"Yes sir, how can I help you?"

"Oh, I didn't push the button," he explained. "There were two women sitting next to me who must have gone to the bathroom. I think they wanted some water."

I could tell by his accent that he was from New York. Smiling, I repeated the word as it sounded to my Texan ears— "Whaater?" Though I was merely being friendly, he must have thought I was flirting.

"Hey, are you making fun of my accent?" he said. Then he asked me to have dinner with him sometime.

"Yeah, sure, okay," I said, thinking, *Absolutely not!* The guy was a mess. Why would I want to go out with him? Determined to ignore him for the rest of the flight, I asked another attendant to take care of his needs.

As soon as the plane landed and we cracked the door in Newark, a thought popped into my head: *Give him your number.* It was odd but suddenly that seemed like the right thing to do, so I wrote it on a beverage napkin and handed it to him as he walked off the plane.

Within two weeks Richie and I were having dinner in Manhattan. As soon as we arrived at the restaurant, he made a confession. "When I talked to you on the phone the other day," he said, "I told you I was thirty-five, but I'm really forty."

We were always partying.

Since I was only twenty-eight, I was a little surprised. Had I known his real age, I would have refused to go out with him. But here we were having dinner in a beautiful restaurant and enjoying each other's company. By the third date I was hooked. Something about his personality attracted me. He was cordial and fun to be with, and he treated me so well that I began to wonder if he might be the one.

I wasn't used to dating someone with so much money. Richie worked on Wall Street and had everything anybody could want. You name it and he could afford it. We were always partying, eating out at great restaurants, and getting VIP treatment wherever we went. But after a while I noticed something that bothered me. Richie drank a lot. At the beginning of the night, he would be charming, but then he would turn mean after several drinks. After a while he seemed like an entirely different guy.

I also noticed his habit of looking at other women. At first I didn't take it too seriously. After all, I had youth on my side. I had no idea that Richie's problems ran far deeper than just a casual appreciation of beautiful women.

One night after we'd been dating for about a year and a half, when he was lying on my lap passed out after a night of partying, I noticed text messages from various women on his phone. Suddenly the truth dawned on me. I had gone from one crazy life to another, from the extreme of being controlled by the church to being with a guy who was drunk and cheating on me. This was hardly the life I'd dreamed of when I'd walked away from the church.

Right after that we broke up, and I began struggling with depression again. I had gone from a girl who had it all—a great job, a great guy, and a great life—to a girl who had a hard time getting out of bed for work. When you feel down, you tend to think of every bad thing that has ever happened to you. So that brought me right back to my childhood and the church.

After Richie and I stopped dating, I began going out with one guy after the other, with no strings attached. When you fly all the time you spend a lot of time in different cities with different people and crazy things happen. I let them happen to me.

A little while after Richie and I broke up, a friend who was like family to me in Texas came for a visit. Though she and her husband had left the church for the same reasons I had, they still believed in God.

Though I loved showing her around New York, I felt anxious as soon as she mentioned her desire to attend church on Sunday. "I don't do church anymore," I explained. But she kept asking, so I gave in.

That Sunday we made our way to a church in midtown Manhattan, one that I'd heard about from another flight attendant. Strangely, the sermon that day was about people who had been hurt by religion. There may have been several of us in the service that day, but I couldn't help feeling that my heart was the bull's-eye for that message. I tried hard to hide my tears.

When my friend tried to talk to me about it afterward, I just brushed her off. Blocking things was a coping skill I'd learned as a child. It was my default setting whenever anything got too painful. I was going to block this out too.

Another year went by. By then I was partying like crazy and crossing lines I had promised I would never cross. Though I wouldn't admit it to myself, I felt ashamed because I was having an affair with a married man.

One night while I was working a red-eye flight, I noticed an older gentleman sitting in his seat reading the Bible. Everyone else was sleeping. After crouching beside him to ask if he needed anything, I allowed myself to be drawn into a conversation about God. I remember him telling me that God loved me.

"No, you don't understand," I said. "I've tried God." How could I tell him that for the first twenty-four years of my life I had done my best to live for God but that it just didn't work?

—

How could I tell him that for the first twenty-four years of my life I had done my best to live for God but that it just didn't work?

—

But he was so kind and sincere, and there was something about the gentle way he spoke that sparked some hope inside me.

Though I was still involved with the married man, I felt a growing sense of unease. How had I sunk so low? Finding it increasingly difficult to live with myself, I finally broke it off.

It wasn't long before I began seeing someone else. One morning after a night of partying, I did the walk of shame out of his apartment in Manhattan. It was Sunday morning and the city was almost deserted. Feeling alone and upset about the kind of person I had become, I looked into the sky and thought, *God, where are you? Where are you?*

Instead of getting on a train to Jersey, where I lived, I decided I would find the church my friend and I had attended a year earlier. I certainly wasn't dressed for the occasion. Instead I was wearing a short little party outfit, with smeared makeup and my hair a mess. I didn't care. I had finally decided to take my messed-up self and go to church.

When I arrived an usher escorted me down the aisle to a seat in the second row. Why wasn't he trying to hide me in the back row instead of taking me right up front? Though I didn't know the answer, I knew that I was being accepted just as I was.

I remember nothing about the service except saying to God, *I don't understand my past. I don't understand the church I was raised in. I don't understand why the things that happened to me happened, but I am ready to live for you.* And that was it. Seven years after I had fled the church in Austin, I walked into the arms of Christ.

RICH

—

I had just boarded a plane in Miami heading to Newark. Shortly after I flopped into the window seat, a woman sitting in the same row punched the call button. A little later she and her friend got up to go to the bathroom.

Soon a beautiful blonde flight attendant was standing next to me, asking how she could help. I explained that my seat-mates wanted some water.

"Whaater?" she said, smiling down at me as she reached above my head to turn off the call light.

"Hey, you're not supposed to make fun of the way I talk," I scolded her. "You're a flight attendant and that's not right." Then I invited her to have dinner with me.

When she said a quick yes, I thought, *Wow! That was easy*. Despite my disheveled appearance, she must have figured out, as most women did, that I was a guy with money. I was also a guy with a headache.

I'd spent the last three nights packing as much fun into my so-called business trip as time would allow. For me that meant nonstop drinking and being with a different woman every night. At least I could rest a little on the plane.

As we prepared to land in Newark, I wondered why that cute flight attendant hadn't been back to see me. *What's with that*, I wondered. But as I was walking off the plane, *cha-ching!*

She smiled and handed me a napkin with her phone number on it.

Timiney and I went out often and had a great time together. She didn't know, because I didn't tell her, how badly I'd treated my previous girlfriend. If we argued when we were out on the town, I would kick her out of the hired car and make her find her own way home. It might be two or three in the morning. I didn't care. If she didn't like the way I treated her, I could always move on to the next woman.

—

I knew that no woman would ever make me happy because no woman ever had.

—

For me it was never about the relationship. It was always about the chase. You hook someone's heart and then you move on. I knew that no woman would ever make me happy because no woman ever had. When I was with someone, I was always looking for someone else, always someone else.

From the very beginning, I told Timiney that I would never remarry and that I didn't want any more children. These were non-negotiable.

Three years earlier I'd walked out on my wife and ten-year-old son because I had decided I'd had enough of married life. I no longer wanted to be tied down, and I was determined to win my freedom no matter what it might cost.

It cost plenty. Since we'd already been married for fifteen years, I gave my ex-wife the house and part of my retirement account. I also agreed to pay her a large permanent alimony. I didn't care about the money. I could always make more.

So how did I get to the point that women, booze, and money were all I cared about?

I can't blame a traumatic childhood, because I didn't have one. My parents split up when I was five, so I grew up between two homes—one in Staten Island, where I lived with my mom, and one in Queens, where my dad and his wife lived. As the youngest of three kids, I sometimes felt like an afterthought or a burden, like, "Hey, don't forget to take care of your little brother." Since Mom had to work, I was on my own a lot and that made me feel a little insecure. Still, my childhood was far from terrible.

As a teenager I began experimenting with drinking and drugs. I did every kind of drug I could get my hands on—pot,

Tuinal, quaaludes, acid. But after a few bad experiences, I backed off the harder stuff and stuck with weed.

School was never the highlight of my life, so I was glad when I finally graduated. I got married when I was twenty-two, and shortly after that my older brother offered me a job on Wall Street where he worked.

I loved Wall Street. I started as a runner, doing whatever the boss told me to do. Then I stepped it up by becoming a trading clerk, then a partial partner, and finally a full partner. By then I was driving expensive cars and enjoying a generous expense account. The money just kept pouring in.

—

You throw lavish parties, hire prostitutes, buy drugs. You do whatever it takes.

—

Succeeding on Wall Street was all about bringing in clients. If you've ever seen the movie *The Wolf of Wall Street*—and I don't recommend it—you'll understand the way I was living. You take clients out. You spend money on them so they will give you business. That's the way it works. You throw lavish parties, hire prostitutes, buy drugs. You do whatever it takes. Then you go back to the trading desk the next day and talk about who did what with whom. If you're the rare person who doesn't go along with all the partying, everyone thinks there's something wrong with you.

When Timiney and I were still dating, I hired a DJ and threw her a huge thirtieth birthday party in the loft apartment in Manhattan that my company maintained. There must have been three hundred people there. Shortly after that we broke up.

Afterward I started dating two women—a twenty-eight-year-old and another girl who was only twenty-two. I'd see one in the afternoon and the other at night.

By the time I was forty-two years old, I was living like some clueless teenager, experimenting with mushrooms and Ecstasy and drinking all the time. I was doing whatever I wanted, when-ever I wanted, all day long. I was completely out of control.

I was also seriously depressed.

Is this all there is to life? I wondered. I had everything I wanted: money, booze, drugs, women, expensive cars and homes. What else was there?

Nothing satisfied me. It was harder to get a thrill out of the things that used to please me. By now my life had become depraved and I knew it. I was so disgusted with myself, I thought I might go crazy. I also considered committing suicide.

Despite feeling depressed I kept going into the office, because I had to keep paying for my lifestyle.

One day I began experiencing chest pains. Fearing a heart attack, I checked myself into the hospital. But it was only a panic attack. As I lay in bed, I began thinking how much simpler life would be if I simply went insane. Then I would be institutionalized and someone else could take care of me. My worries would be over.

A while later I began feeling sick, as though I was coming down with the flu. No surprise, since I hadn't been getting much sleep. The surprise came when I discovered it wasn't the flu but shingles. That explained the nasty-looking rash that was spreading across my face and creeping toward my eye.

The pain was terrible and it wouldn't let up. Adding shingles to the picture was more than I could stand. Finally I told my partners I needed time off. Then I called Timiney. I didn't know what else to do. I needed a friend.

TIMINEY

—

After that Sunday in church, my life began to change. I told God I would start attending church regularly but that I would never, under any circumstances, become a member of one. That would be asking too much.

During the service, whenever someone read a particular Bible passage that reminded me of my former church, I would have to force myself to stay put rather than running out the door like I wanted to.

One day a friend invited me to her church. I remember sitting in the balcony as far back as possible. The worship music was so moving and the presence of God so strong that I kept coming back.

Every Sunday I was a basket case. God was wooing me, healing me, helping me to draw close to him. By then I was no longer working as a flight attendant because of an injury I had sustained. That meant I was home alone much of the time. But God was so close to me.

I used to hobble out into the backyard of my apartment building on crutches, holding a Bible and a water bottle. Every day I would read the Bible and spend hours alone with God. During those months he began to heal me of my bitterness and resentment. He also helped me take responsibility for my own bad choices. Looking back I realize that God was laying a strong foundation for my life, healing me and forgiving me and drawing me to himself.

—

God began to heal me of my bitterness and resentment.

—

Sometimes he would be so close that I hardly dared to breathe for fear that doing so might disrupt my sense of his presence.

After a while I did something I said I never would do: I joined the church. Eventually I began assisting one of the pastors on a volunteer basis.

One day I got a text message from a number I didn't recognize. Someone was reaching out to me, but at first I didn't know who it was. *Who is this?* I asked. *It's Richie*, the text said, *and I'm in a really bad spot. Can we talk on the phone?*

I hadn't recognized his number since I'd deleted it from my phone a long time ago.

When he called me I quickly explained that I was no longer the person he had known. I told him how happy I was now that I'd given my life to God.

"Whatever," he said. It was clear that he desperately needed help.

Though I knew I had to be cautious, I started visiting him. When we were together I would pray or read the Bible to him. He didn't seem to mind, probably because he was so low. He couldn't do his washing, shop for groceries, or even pay his bills, so I helped him with all those things. I would write out his checks, and he would sign them.

After about three months he was well enough to return to work. I went back to my life and he went back to his. By then he was dating a new girl.

RICH

—

Because of the way I'd treated her, I knew I had no right calling Timiney. But I was desperate. When she told me she wasn't the same girl I had known and that her life was different now, I said

"Whatever. Good for you." I didn't have the energy to care. I just needed help.

She was good to me—so much better than I deserved—and after a few months I returned to work. Pretty soon I started dating another girl, even though I wasn't in any shape for another relationship. Though I wasn't drinking as much, I was battling all my old demons.

By then my firm was faltering financially because of the recession. My income was way down, but I still had enormous fixed costs—a six-figure alimony payment and mortgage payments on my million-dollar home among them. It seemed that everything was turning south. Things got so bad that I finally decided to walk away from my home.

One day Timiney texted me, inviting me and my girlfriend to a Christmas program at her church. As we watched the story unfold, something inside me just broke. Weeping through the whole program, I went up to the altar afterward. I must have filled out a card with my contact information on it, but when someone called me from the church, I wasn't interested.

By then I was seeing a psychiatrist, who was doing her best to keep me alive. She told me that killing myself wasn't an option because it wouldn't be fair to my son. I thought about all the years I'd lost with him because of my sexual addiction. Even when we were together, I was always thinking of getting away so that I could hook up with another woman. I didn't want to lay suicide on him too.

—

Instead of turning her back on me in disgust, she told me that Jesus was the only one who could help me.

—

Two years after Timiney and I had reconnected, I called her again and invited her out for her birthday. That night I told her every horrible thing I had ever done, just poured it out because she was a friend and I knew I could trust her.

Instead of turning her back on me in disgust, she told me that Jesus was the only one who could help me.

How's God going to help? I thought. *That doesn't make sense. He's up there and I'm down here. How can he change anything in my life?* It just didn't compute.

I refused to go to church. "It's not going to happen," I told her. The truth is, I felt like I was too bad to go to church, as though it might burn down the moment I stepped through the doors. Or maybe God would just strike me dead.

A few months later, still feeling depressed and suicidal, I decided I had nothing more to lose. *Okay, let me just go to church, because nothing else is working.*

TIMINEY
—

When Richie reached out to me a second time, I knew I needed to be careful. I had such a great relationship with God, and I didn't want anyone separating me from him. Every time I visited Richie, which was about once a week, I would ask the Lord to guide my mind and heart.

A lot of women are tempted to think they can "save" the men in their lives. Often they get dragged down in the process. But by the grace of God that wasn't how I thought about Richie. I didn't want to be anything more than a friend.

After he told me everything, it became clearer than ever that no one but Jesus could solve his problems, and I told him so. But he didn't want to hear about God or church, so I didn't push it. Because of my background, I wasn't going to force-feed anyone.

Instead I just prayed, asking God to reveal himself to Richie. And I kept praying. One Saturday when we were together, he told me he wanted to go to church. "Okay," I said, promising to save him a seat on Sunday. But inside I was thinking, *What!?* I was so surprised.

After church Richie invited me to have dinner at his place. I was apprehensive because I didn't know what he was thinking. Maybe he wanted to tell me that church was a big waste of time, that it was just a religious trap I'd fallen into.

RICH

—

Lightning didn't strike that first Sunday at church. I don't remember anything about the service. But when I went home, I opened the Bible and *boom!* Everything I read seemed to come alive. I couldn't stop reading.

Wow! I thought. *This is life. This is speaking to me.* I knew in that moment that God was real and that he was touching my heart.

What a contrast with the past. The Bible had always seemed so foreign to me. Even when Timiney had read it to me, I still didn't get it. It was such a huge book, and I had always hated reading. I had a hard time because of my ADD. But now I couldn't stop.

TIMINEY

—

When I arrived at Richie's I was surprised to see him standing there with an open Bible in his hand.

"This book is amazing," he said. "It tells you how to live."

Every Sunday after that he would be at church, and it was wonderful to watch the transformation that was taking place.

I was never tempted to push him because I knew it was the Holy Spirit's job to help him change. I didn't think it was my responsibility to do anything but be an example.

As the old Richie slipped away, a new Richie began to emerge. Everything I had liked about him before was still there, but in place of that hard-nosed guy was a man with a much bigger heart, someone who was growing increasingly concerned about the needy, especially homeless people. Meanwhile he continued to devour the Bible and was always reading books about faith.

One Sunday in the midst of the service, while Richie was worshipping God, I looked at him and thought about the kind of man he was becoming. *Uh-oh*, I thought, realizing I was developing feelings for him again. I had no idea how he felt about me. Was I anything more than a friend?

—

**I had no idea how he felt about me.
Was I anything more than a friend?**

—

One day the two of us went out to Ocean Grove on the Jersey Shore. At the end of a perfect day, Richie turned to me and said, "Maybe God has a purpose for us to be together. I mean,

we have a lot of baggage and you know way too much about me. But maybe he has a plan."

When Richie and I began dating again, we sought counseling from a pastor at church. We had too much history to try to do this on our own. Ten months

Together again in a whole new way

after Richie started going to church, we became engaged, and five months later we were married.

RICH
—

When Timiney and I began dating again, I was still working at my firm. By then the company's financial situation had improved. But I no longer fit in. I wasn't a good Wall Street guy anymore, carousing and getting drunk and then bragging about it the next day. My partners weren't thrilled with the new Richie, and tensions began to develop.

—

I wasn't a good Wall Street guy anymore, carousing and getting drunk and then bragging about it the next day.

—

I didn't know what to do since I'd worked at the company for twenty-three years. One thing I was certain of—other firms wouldn't hire me, because I would have to sign a noncompete clause if I ever left my firm. Though I was the head trader, I wouldn't be able to bring my clients with me. Nor did I have the requisite college degree to start over some-where else.

One morning I woke up with the thought that I should step down as a partner and work with the firm as a consul-tant. I felt an immediate sense of peace. When I told my part-ners they were all for it. Why wouldn't they be? I was walking away from 33 percent ownership in the company. But when we couldn't agree on the terms of a settlement, I went from total peace about my decision to overwhelming fear. How was I going to pay my bills?

Instead of sipping piña coladas in an exotic location, we spent our honeymoon in Ethiopia helping others.

Four days before Timiney and I were going to be married, I cried out to God for his help. *Just praise me,* he seemed to say. So that's what Timiney and I did. We thanked him and praised him for everything he had done in our lives. Later that day my partners offered a buyout I could accept. It wasn't a huge amount, but I could live with it.

Timiney and I spent our honeymoon not in an exotic location sipping piña coladas, but in Ethiopia, helping out on a mission trip. It was what we both wanted to do. What a contrast to the way we used to live, trying to squeeze every last millimeter of happiness from life. Now our joy came from an entirely different focus.

—

Giving my life to God didn't make everything perfect. But it made life possible.

—

Giving my life to God didn't make everything perfect. But it made life possible. It made *real* life possible. It wasn't as though God whisked me out of an emotional prison and then transported me to an island paradise where everything was perfect. Timiney and I still had struggles. She couldn't work because of an injury that required multiple surgeries. And I couldn't find another job.

For two years God kept speaking to me about trusting him and having patience. But that was incredibly hard for a guy who didn't know the meaning of the word. During that time I struggled with bouts of depression, but I also had Timiney encouraging and praying for me. And I kept studying Scripture, praying and doing my best to stay close to God.

Despite how difficult that time was for me, I can look back and see how it was part of God's plan. He just stripped a lot of things from me and then began building me back up.

The enemy was active too, reminding me of all the bad things I'd done, especially the way I'd neglected my son. I had lived a crazy, self-centered life for seven years, and I knew I would never get those years back.

But God helped me to resist Satan's lies and receive his forgiveness. He also helped me mend some fences and start living a whole new life. Everything I had been looking for in life I found in him.

Maybe it's no accident that Timiney accepted Christ seven years after she left her church and that I came to know him seven years after leaving my family. Each of us were on separate journeys that could have ended badly. But thank God for weaving our lives together and redeeming our stories so that we can tell others how good he is.

People are always trying to make the world a better place. They're trying to make *their* world a better place. They don't realize that Jesus is the only one who can make them happy. So they keep doing the things they're programmed to do, running after money, relationships, pleasure. But nothing ultimately satisfies.

If I made $200,000 when I was working on Wall Street, I couldn't wait to make $400,000. If I made $400,000 I couldn't wait to make $600,000. If I made $600,000 I couldn't wait to make a million. But no matter how much money I made, it was never enough.

—

I used to think you had to be in good shape to come to God. But now I realize that we all come broken.

—

I was a nasty guy. I would curse people out. Break things. Yell and scream at traders who worked for me. But I'm not that guy anymore. Thank God, I'm not that guy.

I used to think you had to be in good shape to come to God. But now I realize that we all come broken. We come messed up and sinful. And he accepts us just as we are. That's why Christ died, to deal with our brokenness and sin, to bring us back to the Father.

God loves us even when we aren't living as we should be living, because how can we until he saves us? Let's ask him to save us.

ROBIN'S STORY

ROBIN IS THE GRANDDAUGHTER OF JEWISH ÉMIGRÉS WHO ESCAPED COMMUNIST RUSSIA IN ORDER TO SETTLE IN THE UNITED STATES. EMPLOYED BY A NONPROFIT ORGANIZATION, SHE MAKES HER HOME IN ISRAEL. A FREQUENT TRAVELER, SHE ALWAYS MANAGES TO RESPOND TO LIFE WITH GOOD HUMOR. A RECENT MESSAGE TO FACEBOOK FRIENDS HINTS AT HER ADVENTUROUS LIFESTYLE BY ECHOING A FAMOUS PASSAGE FROM THE PASSOVER SERVICE: "WHY IS THIS NIGHT DIFFERENT THAN ALL OTHER NIGHTS? ON ALL OTHER NIGHTS I SLEEP IN HOTELS, HUTS, HOSTELS, TENTS, HAMMOCKS, SLEEPING BAGS, STRANGERS' GUEST ROOMS, AIRPORT LOUNGES, RED-EYE FLIGHTS, AND FRIENDS' COUCHES *BUT ON THIS NIGHT* I WILL SLEEP IN MY OWN BED." FUN LOVING AND FRIENDLY, SHE TELLS OF A TIME IN HER LIFE WHEN DARKNESS THREATENED TO OVERTAKE HER.

THOUGH MY PARENTS DIVORCED when I was young, and my father slipped out of my life, it never occurred to me that I was missing anything. My grandfather, a man of boundless energy, was exactly the father figure I needed at that time.

I remember hearing how he and my grandmother had escaped persecution in the USSR many years earlier. When the government began closing synagogues, he knew it was time to leave. "Persecution you can tolerate," he would say. "But not being able to worship God—that you can't tolerate."

After leaving Moscow, my grandparents made their way through various countries in the Soviet bloc, each time forging new connections that would help them on the next leg of their journey. They were heading toward the one place in the world they dreamed of living—the holy land, otherwise known as Brooklyn. At that time, New York City had more Jewish people living in it than were in the entire country of Israel.

Years later when they visited Russia—don't ask me how they managed to get past the "iron curtain"—they reconnected with some of our relatives who were still living in Moscow. And when I also traveled to Russia, many years later, family members there were full of stories about their visit. They spoke of my grandparents as the greatest, craziest people they knew. During their visit my grandfather had insisted on going to pray at the synagogue.

—

"Do you fear God, or do you fear the KGB?"

—

"You're crazy," they said. "The synagogue is closed. Plus, the KGB is watching."

"Do you fear God, or do you fear the KGB?" my grandfather asked.

"Both!" they exclaimed.

In the end my grandfather made everyone go and pray— *behind* the synagogue.

At home in Brooklyn he and my grandmother were always helping other Jewish immigrants, having them over for Shabbat dinners and allowing people to stay rent-free on one floor of their three-story home until they got established.

Because we lived with my grandparents after my mother and father divorced, they were like parents to me. Both were super social, loving, and kind. And both had a strong faith in God.

I remember how my grandmother would wake up early and begin to clean the house and cook. In addition to baking cookies, she made lots of traditional Russian and Jewish food, like borscht, chopped liver, and gefilte fish—the kind of food you don't like unless you're lucky enough to have a grandma who made it for you when you were a child.

She was full of life, always laughing, playing cards for pennies with friends, and dancing whenever music was playing.

Like her, my grandfather loved life. With his arm wrapped in the traditional leather straps, he would sit by the window every

Growing up in a traditional Jewish home

day and pray. "Maybe today the Messiah will come," he would say. Gathering with other men for prayer, he would return from the synagogue with stories from the Torah—the first five books of the Hebrew Bible—as though he had just heard them from Moses himself. It was easy to picture myself crossing the Red Sea as I held onto Grandfather's hand.

Like many other families in our neighborhood, we kept kosher, celebrated the feasts, and observed the commandments.

After my mother remarried, we moved out of my grandparents' home and into our own. By the time I got to high school, I had morphed into a teenager who was living with a foot in two different worlds. Friday nights I was celebrating Shabbat, and at school I was obsessed with theater, dance, and clubbing.

On the outside I looked like a decent Jewish girl in honors English who lived with her parents in a nice home on Long Island. But like many of my friends, I was also experimenting with drugs and alcohol.

After high school I entered college in Boston, where I continued to experiment with drugs and alcohol. In New York the clubs closed down at 4:00 or 5:00 in the morning. But closing time in Boston was 1:00 or 2:00 a.m. No problem. I just invited everyone back to my dorm room to keep partying.

On the one hand, I was still observing many of the Jewish traditions, reminding cafeteria staff that Passover was coming and that Jewish students would need a separate space for their kosher foods. On the other hand, my dorm room was party central.

I remember returning to the dorm stoned out of my mind one day. Unfortunately the RA, the person responsible for my hallway in the dorm, was sitting in the lobby. "Listen," I said to the guy who was with me. "Be cool, keep quiet, she won't even know." Then I walked smack into a glass door with the RA looking on.

Friends would laugh with me and say, "You won't eat a lobster, but you'll use cocaine!"

Despite all the partying, I made rules to keep things from getting out of hand. I promised myself I would never drink or do drugs alone. I also promised to indulge only when I was happy and never when I was feeling sad or depressed.

One day my parents called. My mom told me that my grandmother had suffered a heart attack and that I needed to come home as soon as possible.

The next day when my mom and stepdad were driving me home from the airport, I was chatting nonstop, telling them how much I loved college, how many friends I had made, how happy I was.

As we stepped into the house, it suddenly occurred to me that neither of my parents had spoken while we were in the car. *What's going on?* I wondered. Then my mother turned to my stepfather and said, "You tell her."

After a brief silence, he plunged in. There was no easy way to tell me the brutal truth. My grandmother had not suffered a mild heart attack as I had been led to believe.

"Your grandmother," he told me, "was the victim of a homicide."

—

There was no easy way to tell me the brutal truth.

—

It felt as though the sun had just fallen out of the sky, plummeting to earth and exploding my world. How could my sweet, loving grandma have been murdered? She was so full of life, so kind. I would never again feel her lips brush my cheek with a kiss, never again watch her eyes flash with joy as she danced, never again be able to tell her how much I loved her. All that had been ripped away in an instant. I couldn't bear thinking about the violent way in which her life had been taken from her. She was my second mother, and now she was gone.

Out of my mind with grief, I started pacing up and down, wailing and screaming. I was in so much pain that I didn't even know I was screaming.

According to the police my grandmother had been the victim of a "push in." While she was unlocking the door to let herself in, someone pushed in behind her, hit her over the head with a metal pipe, crushed her skull, and killed her. Then he robbed her. Do you know how much money went missing? Seven dollars! I'm sure my grandmother would have given him money had he only asked.

My grandfather wasn't at home at the time. When he learned of her death, he was devastated.

—

**The good news they were so eager to share
had always sounded like bad news to me.**

—

A natural death is bad enough, but when there's a murder in your family, people don't know how to react. Sometimes family and friends keep their distance because the situation feels eerie and uncomfortable and they don't know what to say. But there was a group that stuck with us.

While I was away at college, it seemed that everyone else in my family had become good friends with someone who believed in Jesus. Like our other friends, none of these people knew what to say after my grandmother was murdered. But they stayed close and stood by us anyway.

Before I returned to school a week later, every single one of them felt compelled to share the gospel with me. There was only one problem with that: The good news they were so eager to share had always sounded like bad news to me.

Though New York had a large Jewish population, there was still plenty of anti-Semitism when I was growing up. Sometimes kids would call me and my friends Christ-killers, hitting us or refusing to play with us. I was also aware that my grandparents had been persecuted in Russia because they were Jews. Since we were surrounded by Jewish friends and family, I heard stories about how people had lost loved ones during World War II. If they hadn't suffered under Hitler, they had suffered under Stalin.

I remember visiting my birth father's mother—my Polish grandmother—in the hospital at the end of her life. When I asked why she was crying, she said, "Every doctor and nurse who walks through the door wants to know my family history. They should look at a Jewish woman my age and realize that she doesn't have a family history because her family was torn from her."

Another relative had been out of the country when war broke out in Poland. By the time he returned, no one was left. His mother and father, his brothers and sisters, his school teachers, his doctor, even his mailman—they had all perished for the crime of being a Jew.

Because many people who call themselves Christians look down on Jews, I didn't want to have anything to do with the New Testament. I thought it was the source of anti-Semitism.

Suddenly in the immediate aftermath of my grandmother's murder, I had three or four people every day telling me that Jesus was good news and that he was the Messiah.

Since I would never let them speak about the New Testament, they began pointing out many of the messianic prophecies in the Hebrew Scriptures. But I wasn't interested in probing the Bible to discover the truth. I resisted, not only because of the prejudice against my people, but also because I didn't want anyone telling me that what I was doing in my life was sin. I was entirely hostile to every overture they made.

Despite my resistance, when I returned to school I couldn't stop thinking about all the Scripture passages they pointed out. Who were they about? Because of my grandmother's death, anxiety often kept me up until 4:00 or 5:00 a.m. anyway, so I had plenty of time to think.

Six months after my grandmother was killed, my grandfather passed away. I think he died of a broken heart. As for me, I was no longer the fun-loving, outgoing party girl. Instead of going out all the time, I stayed home. A year before my grandmother's death, my brother's best friend and his mother had been killed in a violent crime that had made the headlines in Long Island. These tragic events created an overwhelming cloud of fear and sadness.

—

With my sense of security ripped away, I began breaking the rules I had made for myself.

—

With my sense of security ripped away, I began breaking the rules I had made for myself, drinking and doing drugs when I was alone and when I was feeling sad or angry. Though

I wasn't an addict, I was abusing drugs and alcohol. I was also beginning to feel ill—very ill. You know you're sick when your drug dealer refuses to sell you any more drugs out of concern for you, as mine did. At that point I decided no more drugs and alcohol for me.

My illness started with weight loss and fatigue. As the months passed, my skin began to bleed, the whites of my eyes turned bright yellow, and my hair started coming out in clumps. No matter how much rest I got, I had no energy. By the time I quit college and moved home, my five-foot-ten frame was down to skin and bones.

My parents took me to the best doctors they could find. But no one could help me. I had hepatitis and my blood was toxic. My kidneys were failing, my heartbeat was irregular, and I would sometimes pass out because my blood pressure was so low. Lab technicians wanted to meet me because they couldn't believe a person whose blood was so toxic could still be walking around.

Desperate to help me, my mother sent me to an alternative health center, hoping their brand of spirituality and healthy eating would cure me.

One woman caught my attention. I couldn't help noticing how different she was from everyone else. She had come to the center to learn to cook health food and was surprised when she realized it was guided by a New Age philosophy. While she was there, she spent a lot of time reading a particular book. When I questioned her about it, she told me it was her Bible. She hadn't spoken to me about her faith because she knew I was Jewish, and she didn't want to offend me. After that, I literally forced her to share the gospel with me. Everything she said about Jesus and about love, forgiveness, and peace attracted me. A tiny opening was beginning to take shape in my heart.

—

Everything she said about Jesus and about love, forgiveness, and peace attracted me.

—

But I was too sick to stay there. So I found myself at home again. My mom had recently gotten back in touch with a high school friend—a Jewish woman who believed Jesus was the Messiah. She would visit us nearly every day, and each day she would say the same thing to me: "I want to take you to church. We'll pray for you and God will heal you."

I would respond by assuring her that I would never in my life set foot in a church. Why would I want to? Some of the neighborhood churches had Jesus hanging on a cross outside. I couldn't imagine why anyone would believe that a dead person could be God. Of course I knew nothing about the resurrection.

But my mother's friend wouldn't give up. I told her I didn't mind speaking with her about Jesus as long as she never mentioned the New Testament. So she focused on messianic prophecies from the Hebrew Scriptures and highlighted how the Jewish holidays, especially Passover, pointed to Jesus.

I would argue with her every day, but she never met my anger with anger. Instead she would say, "I guess we've had enough for today." Then she would go home and pray for God to change my heart enough for her to be able to come back the next day.

One day she read a passage from her Bible:

He was despised and rejected by mankind,

a man of suffering, and familiar with pain.

Like one from whom people hide their faces

he was despised, and we held him in low esteem.

Surely he took up our pain

and bore our suffering,

yet we considered him punished by God,

stricken by him, and afflicted.

But he was pierced for our transgressions,

he was crushed for our iniquities;

the punishment that brought us peace was on him,

and by his wounds we are healed.

We all, like sheep, have gone astray,

each of us has turned to our own way;

and the Lord has laid on him

the iniquity of us all.

———

The passage she was reading was so obviously about Jesus that I fell into a rage. "I would like you to leave and never come back," I said. "Because now I know what you've been doing. You've been sneaking in passages from the New Testament. I haven't been able to sleep because I've been spending so much time thinking about all the things we've talked about, but now I know that you've been deceptive."

"Okay," she said. "But one thing before I go." Heading over to the cabinet where we kept some of my grandparents belongings, she pulled out the family Bible. Opening it to Isaiah 53:3-6, she passed it to me and said, "Read it for me from your own book."

—

**"I don't know what's happening to me,
but I feel like I had chains on me and
they just fell off. It's like I was sleeping
my entire life and I just woke up, like new
blood is running inside me. I feel alive!"**

—

I couldn't believe it. My Bible was talking about Jesus. As I read from the Hebrew Scriptures, a clear picture of Jesus began to emerge. Everything we had talked about came together, and I realized that Jesus is the Messiah the Jewish people have always been waiting for.

The next day I went to church with her. After the sermon I went up for prayer. Her faith in what God intended to do was so strong that she fully expected me to be healed on the spot. She felt certain I would gain twenty to thirty pounds and that my skin tone would immediately improve. But when she looked at me after I'd received prayer, she saw somebody who was still a mess.

As she started to walk away, I called out to her. "I don't know what's happening to me, but I feel like I had chains on me and they just fell off. It's like I was sleeping my entire life and I just woke up, like new blood is running inside me. I feel alive!"

Running back, she exclaimed, "You just met Yeshua—you met Jesus!" Pointing first to my head and then to my heart, she said, "Yesterday it was here, but now it's here."

And she was right. As soon as I got home I started reading the New Testament. I couldn't put it down. What blew me away was to see how loving Jesus was. I wept through the Gospels.

I was amazed by how Jewish the New Testament is. I already knew Jesus was Jewish. But no one told me that Matthew, Mark, John, Peter, Paul, and almost everyone else was also Jewish. These people were like my own family. They talked about the same things we did. They went back and forth to the temple. They celebrated the holidays. Most shocking of all was the scene in the book of Acts in which the leaders of the early church discussed whether Gentile believers would need to be circumcised. In other words, did they need to become Jews?

The answer was no, but I was amazed that the question was even asked!

Though I was still very ill, I decided to attend a neighborhood church. The first day, I sat in the back, hoping no one would talk to me. When a guy came up and greeted me, I said, "I'm Jewish and I just kind of want to sit here and listen."

"I'm Jewish too," he said. Before I knew it I was surrounded by Jewish people who believed in Jesus. It seems I had wandered into the perfect church for me.

I was still too sick to work or go to school, but I could read my Bible and pray, and many people in the church prayed with me. There were a lot of things in my life, both physical and emotional, that needed Jesus' healing.

When I first began to pray, a lot of ugly emotions came to the surface. There was so much bitterness, shame, fear, and anger. As I kept praying, the Lord led me to pray for the person who had killed my grandmother. I prayed for hours. As the bitterness and hate bubbled up, I felt prompted to ask what had happened in this person's life that could push him to kill a grandma. I began to weep for him and to pray that he would know God's healing and love. It is the most freeing thing when you can forgive someone the way God has forgiven you. Only Jesus could help me do that.

Then I began bringing God all the guilt and shame I felt for everything I had done wrong in my life. As I prayed and read and memorized Scripture, fear began to drop off me, and God released me from the hatred I felt for others.

Jesus began by lifting the heaviest stones first, the ones that had lodged in my heart and dragged me down. Then one by one he removed the smaller stones. With no more shame or guilt or unforgiveness, I felt free for the first time in my life.

—

As I prayed and read and memorized Scripture, fear began to drop off me, and God released me from the hatred I felt for others.

—

Though my heart was growing lighter, my body was still weighed down by illness. I wasn't getting worse, but I wasn't getting any better. One morning while a guest preacher was speaking, I felt God tugging at me with a message. *Go up and ask for prayer, and I will heal you.*

Uh, no, I thought. *There are too many people for me to go up there. I'll go tonight.* The evening service would have fewer people, many of whom I knew. It wouldn't feel as awkward because they would understand why I was going up for prayer.

But his voice was insistent. *Go up and ask for prayer. I'm going to heal you.*

So I did what I didn't want to do. I got up in front of everyone and asked for prayer.

The next day I checked in to the lab for my weekly blood work. Two days later, my doctor told me, "They mixed up your blood at the lab. We'll have to redo it."

When I returned to the doctor's office after the second

blood draw had been analyzed, the nurse looked at me strangely. "What happened?" she asked.

"What do you mean, 'What happened?'" I didn't know what she was talking about.

"Didn't the doctor tell you?" Without waiting for an answer, she ushered me into his office.

I felt free for the first time in my life.

"Robin, what happened?" he asked. "Your blood work came back normal. It wasn't toxic at all."

He explained that even though hepatitis leaves a permanent marker in your blood, there was no marker in mine. That's why he thought the lab had mixed up the specimens.

—

"I don't have a history," I told him. "God healed me."

—

When I told him that Jesus had healed me, he was quiet for a moment. Then he said, "Three times I have seen something that science can't explain. I don't know what I believe, but all three times the people who have experienced these things have told me the same thing you did."

Many years later, in preparation for overseas travel, another doctor wanted me to undergo a series of tests because of my history with hepatitis. "I don't have a history," I told him. "God healed me."

"Just do it for me," he urged.

So I did, and the results of all three tests—a liver scan, a sonogram, and blood work—came back negative. "You have the liver of a twenty-year-old!" he exclaimed.

"A twenty-year-old frat boy?" I quipped.

"No, even with no history of hepatitis, people your age usually have scars and marks on their livers, but yours is perfectly clean. There's not a mark."

After I went up for prayer that day in church, I began to gain weight, my skin started to improve, and my thin hair began to thicken. I felt great. For the first time in nearly three years, I had the energy to think about what I would do with the rest of my life. The first thing I wanted to do was go to Israel.

Because my family already had Jewish friends who believed in Jesus, they didn't have a particularly difficult time adjusting to my beliefs. To my surprise and delight, I learned that even my grandparents may have become believers before their deaths.

But in Israel things were different. One of my cousins sent me to a deprogrammer to un-brainwash me from believing in Jesus. Instead of destroying my faith, it made me stronger.

Sometimes people make the mistake of thinking that if you believe in Jesus you have left your Jewish heritage behind.

But the truth is that I never stopped being Jewish. I am simply a Jew who believes that Jesus is the Messiah.

I used to think a life connected to God would be boring. That it would constrict and confine me. But I have found it to be the greatest adventure of all. There's a reason why Jesus is determined to set us free. When there's no fear or shame or bitterness to hold us back and weigh us down, then anything is possible.

—

I never stopped being Jewish. I am simply a Jew who believes that Jesus is the Messiah.

—

I believe that the same God who delivered his people by parting the Red Sea will make a way for us, no matter what we are facing. He is the one who says,

> The Lord your God is with you,
>> the Mighty Warrior who saves.
> He will take great delight in you;
>> in his love he will no longer rebuke you,
>> but will rejoice over you with singing.
> (Zephaniah 3:17)

KAITLIN'S STORY

———

KAITLIN PINKLETON HAS SPENT MOST OF HER LIFE LIV-
ING IN SOUTHERN STATES, FIRST IN SOUTH CAROLINA AND
THEN IN FLORIDA. A FORMER DRUG AND ALCOHOL COUN-
SELOR, SHE NOW WORKS WITH YOUTH IN NEW YORK CITY.
SHE GREW UP LISTENING TO STORIES OF A STORM THAT
WREAKED HAVOC IN CHARLESTON, SOUTH CAROLINA,
WHERE SHE AND HER MOTHER LIVED. YEARS LATER, FACING
HER OWN PERSONAL STORMS, SHE SPENT THREE DAYS ON A
BUS TRYING TO ESCAPE THE HAVOC THAT WAS THREATENING
HER LIFE.

HURRICANE HUGO SLAMMED into South Carolina when I was only a toddler. I remember nothing of the rain streaking horizontally across the sky, or the chunks of debris that flew past our windows. Nor do I remember the water breaching Charleston's downtown seawall or the blue lightning low in the sky that was not lightning at all but power lines arcing when trees fell across them. When I walk down the streets of Charleston today, I can't recall the swampy smell that filled the air from all the tree debris that covered the ground like snow.

Like many other residents, my mom and I had fled the hurricane in advance, taking shelter out of harm's way. What I do remember are all the stories people told. How the monster storm terrorized anyone who remained in the city, toppling buildings and tossing boats around like toys. When it was all over, Charleston looked like a war zone. Hugo had caused so much damage it would take the aching city years to recover.

That storm is a metaphor for my life.

When I look back on that time, I see myself as a shy little girl with curly blond hair who loved to dress up and play dolls almost as much as she liked digging in the dirt for roly-polies, little bugs that roll up tight whenever they feel threatened. I remember playing with my dog in the yard, dressing up like Raggedy Ann for Halloween, and swinging my small fist at a tetherball as it wrapped wildly around a pole. Like any child, I was curious, playful, and eager to explore the world around me. I was unaware of the approaching storm.

I didn't know that my mother was dealing with gale force winds in her own life because my father had been seeing another woman and wanted out of the marriage. They divorced when I was only two. After that it was just my mom and me trying to make a life together because

A shy little girl

my dad had erased us from his. Though he never got in touch, I tried establishing a small connection once by sending him a Father's Day card. But he sent it back unopened. I was seven years old.

Though Mom kept trying to better herself, taking classes and working multiple jobs, she had a tough time of it. She had lost her own parents when she was ten. And they had been alcoholics. After that her sister tried raising her, but it's hard for a sibling to take on that responsibility. I think Mom's upbringing left holes in her life that were never filled.

She tried plugging the holes with men—a long succession of boyfriends who would either live with us or invite us to live with them. None of these relationships lasted more than a couple of years because the kind of men she attracted were as unstable as she was. They never stuck around.

I was four years old when "Tom" came along. At first he seemed like a nice guy, like somebody who might make a good daddy. We were living in Tom's first-floor apartment and hoping to move to one upstairs. My mom was busy fixing up the second-floor apartment so we could live there. One night Tom offered to put me to bed so she could keep working on the apartment. I remember my bed—a pull-out couch in the living room—and Tom lifting me up and then setting me on his lap. But it wasn't in a tender way, like a father holding his child before tucking her in for the night. Instead of hugging me and reading me a bedtime story, he raped me.

Though I didn't understand what had happened, I knew it was wrong, and I blamed myself for the terrible pain I felt. When my mom came down that night, I told her my vagina hurt. But I couldn't explain what had taken place and she didn't put two and two together.

The abuse went on for the next few years. Every night Mom would tuck me into bed, read me a story, and tell me she loved me. As soon as she closed the door, I would hide under the covers, bunching my blankets up and piling toys and stuffed animals around me. Maybe Tom wouldn't notice me when he came in; maybe he would think I was just blankets or toys and leave the room. But it never happened that way. After we finally moved out, Mom would drop me off at his place so he could babysit while she was at work. Whenever she left me alone with him, I would scream and cry, but she just thought I was upset because I was missing her. So the nightmare continued.

Tom had some small dogs at his house, and he would threaten to hurt them if I told anyone what he was doing to me. He would give me candy to shut me up. Or he would threaten to kill my mom. The fear of what he might do kept me quiet for a long time.

By the time I was seven, the pain had become so unbearable that I blurted out the truth to my mom one day. As soon as she heard what was happening, she called the police. But it took a while to get a conviction.

Even though Tom's secret was out in the open, I was still terrified. While he awaited trial, he lurked around the school playground, just outside the fence. I wanted to go to school, to learn and to do whatever a normal child would do. I thought recess would be fun. But Tom was always outside, pacing up and down and staring at me as I played ball. I did my best to act normal even though I knew I wasn't. Why else would he be stalking me, unless I was different from all the other kids? I was so afraid, so terrified of what he was going to do to me.

I was especially scared he would follow me home after school. One day I got spanked for walking to a girlfriend's house without telling my mom. Finally I told her I was afraid to go home by myself.

Eventually the trial went forward, and Tom was sentenced to two years in prison. But even after Tom was locked up, I felt no peace. I was devastated by everything that had happened— the years of abuse, the doctors examining me, the never-ending counseling sessions the court recommended.

I'm sure it nearly destroyed my mother when she realized what had taken place under her nose. But I was glad that she stood up for me when the truth finally came out.

When I look back on that seven-year-old who had lost her daddy and fallen into the hands of a sexual predator, I sometimes find it hard to stop the tears from coming. No wonder that little girl felt so empty, so isolated, so broken by the storms of life that just kept coming, one after the other.

—

No wonder that little girl felt so empty, so isolated, so broken by the storms of life that just kept coming.

—

Since Mom worked the night shift, I was either with babysitters or home alone. It wasn't a good life for either of us, and it filled me with fear and a sense of instability. Mom became so depressed that she would sleep on the couch from the time she came home to the time she got ready for work.

Because I felt different than other kids, I had trouble making friends. Since there wasn't much structure at home, I would head off on in search of adventure, just riding my bike for hours and hours. I'd chase cats through town and wander through the woods by myself. I'd go into other kids' yards and start jumping on their trampolines while their parents were inside watching me. I'm sure they wondered what I was doing in their backyards and why I was always on my own.

Sometimes Mom and I would go to church, and I loved that. It was so different than the rest of my life, because there was so much love in that place. I think she was trying to get herself together and make a better life for the two of us. We spent lots of time at the pastor's house, just hanging out.

At one point when I was about ten, she started seeing a guy who worked at a fair. She had just lost her job, so he invited us to travel with him. We packed up a few things and moved to North Carolina. I thought it was fun, because what kid doesn't like hanging around fairs and malls, eating free popcorn? But after a while, moving from town to town became lonely and boring. I'd start new schools and then leave and then start over again.

After about six months of this, my mom and her boyfriend had a terrible argument in a hotel room. He attacked her and we fled. But we had no money and no place to go. So there we were in North Carolina in the middle of winter, living out of our car.

Because she didn't know what else to do, Mom finally called her sister in Florida, the one who had raised her, and asked if we could stay with her for a while. That's when we moved to West Palm Beach. Mom and I slept together on the top bunk in my three-year-old cousin's room. But there was a lot of stress in my aunt's house too.

I remember thinking that my aunt and my cousins treated my mom like Cinderella's stepmother and stepsisters had treated her. Of course, no fairy godmother or handsome prince ever showed up to rescue her.

Every time there was a fight, we'd move out. That meant changing schools. Then we would move back in again, because Mom would run out of money. By the time I was nineteen, we had moved thirty-four times.

Finally she met a guy she really liked. Maybe this one would stick around. Instead he fell ill and died. After that she spiraled into a deep depression. Both of us moved out of my aunt's house, and I began staying with a friend's family. I was thirteen years old. My friend's parents tried to get me into sports and involve me in school activities, but I was hard to help. I wasn't used to living in a healthy home where there was a lot of structure, even though I needed it.

—

By the time I was sixteen, I was out of control and running wild.

—

When I was fourteen I started sleeping with boys and partying. If someone brought drugs to a party, I was the first to sample them. I tried ecstasy and then settled on weed and cocaine. By the time I was sixteen, I was out of control and running wild. Nobody knew how to get through to me. By then I had become a full-blown addict.

I was out of control and running wild.

I don't know how, but I managed to hold down a job at an Italian restaurant for the next few years. That job was the only stable thing in my tempestuous life.

After a while Mom got it together a little, and I moved back in with her. She was upset that I wasn't attending high school, so I started to homeschool myself. She also wanted my father to pay child support. But Dad was still living in South Carolina, and he wasn't interested in giving us anything. He hired a private investigator in Florida to follow me around in order to document for the court that I had a job and money and therefore didn't need any of his.

It felt like someone had always been following me. When I was little, Tom had stalked me on the playground. Now it was my father and his private detective. Somehow I began to think that God must be watching me too. I could almost see the frown on his face as he waited for me to mess up.

When the court took up the case, Mom and I had to return to South Carolina. Going home brought back lots of memories, most of them painful. Surprisingly, when I spotted my father in court that day, I felt no hatred. I was just curious about the man I resembled. Who was he? What was his life like? I wondered about my half-sister too. That side of the family was a complete mystery to me.

When we returned to West Palm Beach, things got worse. I kept buying drugs and drinks for everyone, partying and passing out. I was dressing provocatively, always attracting the wrong kind of guy. I had such a low opinion of myself that I assumed my body was something for someone else to use. I was manipulative and deceitful and not above stealing to get what I wanted. That was my life for the next few years.

In the midst of all the craziness, I still managed to think of myself as a good girl. For a long time I played the part, holding down several jobs. Whenever someone noticed that things weren't okay with me, I would shift the blame to my boyfriend. People would feel sorry for me because it was my "bad boyfriend" who was bringing me down.

By then I was living with a disc jockey, a man five years older than I was, who had spent a lot of time in and out of jail. After drinking and drugging, we'd get into fights. I'd hit back but he would always get the better of me.

Whenever things got really rough, I'd go back to my mom's house. Then she'd get sick of me and throw me out. Soon I'd be back with the boyfriend. Then we would both start living with her. It was a vicious cycle.

When I hurt myself at work, my boyfriend introduced me to prescription pain pills. OxyContin, Percocet, Vicodin, you name it. It was pretty much medical-grade heroin, and I was completely addicted to it.

Pretty soon I was frequenting crack houses and looking for doctors to feed my pill habit. Since I could no longer hold down a job, I sold extra pills for five or ten dollars each—anything for a little money.

Whenever I didn't have drugs to pop in my mouth, I felt sick. I'd lie in bed for days, suffering from withdrawal. For a year I was in and out of detox centers with nothing to show for it.

I moved back in with my mom and started seeing a guy who was fourteen years older than me. By then Mom was drinking too. One day she threw me out, screaming, "Enough is enough! I can't take it anymore. You're my daughter, but I don't know who you are. You've become a monster!"

And she was right. Inside I was a little monster, enraged and full of pain, with not even a shred of hope. Now I had nowhere to go. I'd already tired out everyone I knew, begging to sleep on their couch for just a few days. But there were no more couches to sleep on.

There was, however, a shed in an empty lot down the street. Pushing aside the cigarette butts, gasoline containers, and old clothes that were stored inside, I made it my home for the next couple of months. In that dark place, with nowhere to go and no one to help me, I began to wonder how I had sunk so low. I was twenty-two years old. Though I had my whole life ahead of me, I felt I was already reaching the end. Incredibly, I still thought of myself as a good girl who'd had some bad luck. But there was no denying how sad my wretched life had become. If I'd had more guts, I would have killed myself.

—

There was no denying how sad my wretched life had become. If I'd had more guts, I would have killed myself.

—

For the first time in my life, I was beginning to admit the devastation caused by the hurricane that was my life. I desperately wanted to get away from the pain I could no longer endure, but I didn't know how. Maybe if I left Florida behind, I could get better. I knew about a local church that met on the beach and did its best to help the homeless. They bought me a one-way ticket to New York to enter a treatment program headquartered in the city.

When I told my mom I was leaving, she was furious. "You mean you're gonna leave me here with your mess, and you're gonna leave the state?" Despite how painful and twisted our lives had become, I still loved her, and I wanted to think she still loved me. But now the alcohol was talking. She was so angry that she started hitting me, and I hit back. Finally the cops came and arrested her.

Now I had nothing left. No job, no boyfriend, and no mom. She was so upset and hurt that she didn't want me in her life. That's when I cried out to God, begging for his help.

"God, you have to help me," I sobbed. "I'll go anywhere you want, I'll do anything you want. Just help me, please!"

So with ten dollars in my pocket, I boarded a bus and headed north. The three-day journey from Palm Beach to New York City was an emotional roller coaster, allowing me time to think about my life. I wasn't sure if I could get sober or that I even wanted to. But I was afraid of doing drugs on the streets of New York, because I didn't know how the game was played there.

I got off the bus at Forty-Third Street and Eighth Avenue, in the midst of a world that was nothing like Florida. I was so desperate that I flagged down the closest policeman. "I'm a drug addict," I said. "I need to find this program." Then I gave him the address and he told me how to get there.

From that point on everything changed. At the age of twenty-three, I entered a treatment program that was run like the army. I stopped smoking and taking drugs. Though I'd had so few rules and so little structure in my life, I warmed to the atmosphere because it made my life feel far less crazy.

As part of the program I went back to school and got a degree in counseling. I also hooked up with a fifty-year-old guy who was in the program. It was such an obvious pattern. I was dating older and older men in search of a father figure, someone to watch over me.

The program encouraged everyone to get involved in some kind of spiritual belief system. There were outings to monasteries, Buddhist centers, Catholic churches, and yoga classes. Of course there was also Narcotics Anonymous and Alcoholics Anonymous. I tried everything, from crystals to chakras. Though I wasn't doing drugs, I was still empty, still broken, still looking for God but not knowing where to find him.

On the outside I looked pretty good. No longer homeless and helpless, I had a job as a drug and alcohol counselor, money in the bank, and a relationship—all the things that are supposed to make you happy. But I was still in a dark place.

Toward the end of the two-and-a-half year program, I sustained a serious injury as a result of a freak accident. Now I didn't even have my health to rely on. It felt as though another storm was bearing down, threatening to undo all the progress I had made. But I was wrong about that.

One day a friend invited me to a church in downtown Brooklyn. I went because why wouldn't I? Hadn't I already been to every kind of church you could imagine?

This one was different. As soon as I walked in, I felt at home. Though it was much larger than the church I attended as a child, it reminded me of the love I'd felt back then. So I kept going back, kept leaning over the balcony of the old-theater-turned-church, not wanting to miss out on a single word. Whenever the choir sang, I felt like I was being wrapped up in something beautiful, something holy.

My boyfriend came to church with me, but he wasn't enthusiastic; he didn't want to change the way things were.

I remember attending a New Year's Eve service where everyone was singing and praising God. I had never been in a place where you could be sober and experience so much joy. As I joined in the worship, I felt God touching my heart, filling me up. I gave my life to Christ in that moment, telling him once again that I would go wherever he wanted and do whatever he wanted. I felt forgiven, washed clean, loved. The Father of the fatherless was there with me, healing me, taking my depression, my isolation, my fear, my hurts—everything—and replacing them with his peace. That's when God really got hold of me.

—

The Father of the fatherless was there with me, healing me, taking my depression, my isolation, my fear, my hurts.

—

I realized then that I had a choice to make. My boyfriend and I were still intimate, even though I knew it wasn't right. I also knew he wasn't interested in changing his life or in helping me with my health problems. Still it was very difficult to break off, because he was my security blanket, the first guy I had dated in New York, and someone I had thought I wanted to marry. But now it was clear that I couldn't have him and have God too.

It was a real battle to let go. Fortunately I began making friends at church. These weren't the kind of friends who would say, "Hi, how you doing?" and then keep walking. They really wanted to know. They took me to doctors' appointments, bought me lunch, and picked me up for church. They also told me the truth, pointing out the lies I was tempted to believe—that I was no good, that I could never be happy, that I didn't deserve to be loved. They told me God was the Father I had always been looking for and that he could help me and heal me.

At this time I was easing out of the program. My doctor was encouraging me to find ways to integrate back into society. "You don't need all these therapies anymore," he said. "Why don't you volunteer more at your church?"

During my journey out of drug addiction, I had prayed for God to hem me in, to keep me from running, to prevent me from returning to that crazy life. He answered my prayer in so many ways. Today I've got girlfriends, father figures, and men who feel like brothers to me. I have everything I need because of how faithful God has been. For the last seven years I've been completely free from drugs. I am not the person I used to be.

But it's not all about me. As God has healed me, he has also given me something to do. I volunteer with young people, some of whom have lived through their own tough times.

Because I've been there, I know what they're up against. I also know what God can do.

Though he has made my life rich and fruitful, it hasn't been easy. My health issues are an ongoing challenge. But they don't throw me. Instead of seeing them as another threatening storm, I view my difficulties as one more chapter of my story. At the beginning there were lots of hard chapters, full of misery. But even in the midst of difficulty, this new chapter feels different because I know God is in control. I trust him to bring good out of every hard thing.

Whenever I meet someone who has suffered from sexual abuse, I tell them it's not their fault. I also tell them their past does not need to control their future.

If you ask Christ, he will heal you. He will give you back your life, not erasing the past but using it for his glory so that you will no longer need to be afraid. You don't have to feel like a failure. You don't need to be plagued by insecurity and doubt. There is hope. God will walk with you through the painful moments and heal you, and you will come out stronger. Your scars will turn into warrior stripes, and God will make you a blessing to somebody.

Because of what I've been through, I know that Jesus is good at restoring people. There's a verse in the Bible that says he will repay us for the years the locusts have eaten. That's

—

God will walk with you through the painful moments and heal you, and you will come out stronger.

—

exactly what's happened in my life. The hurricane that nearly destroyed me so many years ago, leaving behind a trail of chaos and brokenness, is only a memory now. Because God has come and healed my aching heart.

But what about the other people in my story? How do I feel about them?

I don't blame my mother for what happened, not for a moment. I know she did the best she could against very challenging odds, and I love her for that. I also love her for standing up for me once she knew about the abuse. I understand how difficult her own life was from a very early age. I realize that brokenness has a way of threading itself through generations. Now that I am better, it would be tempting to play the therapist, to develop a treatment plan for her, to be her savior. In fact I have tried to do all those things. But it doesn't work. The only one who can do that is Jesus. And I believe he will.

What about my father? God has given me the grace to see that he is what we all are—a sinner in need of grace and restoration. Whether I ever get the chance to talk to him about what happened—and I would like to talk to him—I want him to know that I forgive him, that I care about him, and that I want him to be happy.

As good as it is, the healing I have experienced doesn't stop there. Jesus has also given me the desire to tell Tom, the man who abused me when I was a little girl, that I forgive him too.

The Bible says that the light shines in the darkness, and the darkness has not overcome it. That means that light is stronger than darkness. Because of what's happened in my life, I know these are not just words on a page. They are the truth. Anyone who follows Jesus will not walk in darkness, but will have the light of life.

ALEX'S STORY

———

ALEXANDER COLON IS A CONSTRUCTION AND ENGINEER-ING SUPERVISOR AT A NONPROFIT ORGANIZATION. HE GREW UP IN BROOKLYN, THE FIFTH OF SEVEN CHILDREN. A LIKEABLE TOUGH GUY, HE WOULD BE THE FIRST TO TELL YOU THAT HE SHOULDN'T BE ALIVE TO SHARE HIS STORY.

IT IS THREE IN THE MORNING and I am drunk. I have already passed beneath the shadow of the Verrazano-Narrows Bridge, driving home along Brooklyn's Belt Parkway. Between exits 3 and 4 the road bends outward just enough to skirt Dyker Beach Park. After that it swings back to shore and then veers left as it approaches exit 5.

The last thing I remember before I fall asleep is exit 4, two exits from Gravesend. With the Upper New York Bay to my right and oncoming traffic to my left, I am no longer driving the car. When I wake up, I am a mile down the road, heading straight toward exit 5, where I usually get off. I am stunned. How has my car managed to stay in the lane even though the road veered left? And how did I wake up just in time to exit the parkway? I should be floating in the bay right now or crushed by oncoming traffic. Yet I am still alive. I pull to the side of the road and cover my face with my hands. I can't stop the flood of tears that rushes down my cheeks. I sit there a long time, wondering what just happened. Whose hand was steering the wheel while I slept?

Despite my narrow escape on the parkway, nothing in my life changed. I drove home and kept living like I always had.

It didn't occur to me until much later that my experience that night pretty much summed up my life. In some mysterious way God was keeping me alive, even though I should have been dead a long time ago.

———

Born in Brooklyn, I come from a large Puerto Rican family, the fifth of seven children. Until I was five, I thought my dad was a pretty cool guy. A drummer with piercing blue eyes and dark hair, he could play all kinds of instruments. He was handsome and charming, and people seemed to gravitate to him. I felt lucky to have such a dad, until I started noticing how often his friends had to carry him home dead drunk from the bar.

Macho to the nth degree, he would make my brother and me sit down at the table so my mom and five sisters could serve us. Whenever we tried to help them, he got angry.

Dad always had a cigarette in one hand and a bottle of beer in the other. If he noticed me looking at him, he'd say, "If I ever see you smoking or drinking, I'm gonna give you such a beating."

Whenever he got drunk, which was all the time, he would fight with my mom, beating her and throwing her around while my brother and sisters and I huddled in the corner crying.

Unlike my five sisters and my brother, I gave both of my parents plenty of trouble. In those days they didn't know what to do with kids like me except to beat on them. Today I would probably be diagnosed with ADD . . . or LMNOP, you name it, all the way to Z.

Whenever my dad called me "Alexander," rather than "Alex," I knew I was in for it. He would take off his belt and whip me or roll up his sleeves and hammer me with his fists. Instead of making me meeker, his beatings cut me inside and made me calloused. Hard as nails and numb to the pain, I just took it.

"You're stupid! You're dumb!" he would shout, over and over, until I began to believe it.

When you're a kid you think your father is your protector. But mine never fought for us, never tried to help us. Instead he just got drunk and then brought a lot of fear into the house. As a child you become cold, you become hard. I mean, a kid shouldn't be thinking about how he can get rid of his father. That shouldn't be in his mind. But I thought about it all the time.

When it came to work, my father never did the same thing for very long. He took a lot of odd jobs in construction and factories. For a while he managed a movie theater. But he was never much of a provider.

—

A kid shouldn't be thinking about how he can get rid of his father. That shouldn't be in his mind. But I thought about it all the time.

—

Because of his alcoholism, he wasn't close to any of his children. When I was nine my oldest sister swallowed a bunch of pills and took her life. Part of me blamed my father for her death, because he never seemed to care about her. Maybe it was because she was my mom's daughter by a previous relationship.

I'll never forget coming home after my sister's funeral. Dad was playing his beloved salsa music full blast as though he was at a party. He acted like nothing had happened. My mom was so furious that she ripped the arm off the turntable, and that started another war. My siblings and I hid in another room until things quieted down. I tried to shut out the screaming and yelling, but I couldn't stop thinking about what my dad was doing to my mom in the next room.

When that's the kind of home you live in, you learn not to talk about it. You don't tell your cousins, your uncles, your aunts, or anyone else about what's going on in your house. You just keep quiet and bottle everything up inside.

My mom was the opposite of my dad. She was always taking care of everybody, cooking for everyone, trying her best to keep us together. She didn't deserve a husband like that. Finally, when I was about eleven, she got the guts to throw Dad out of the house. Since he was no longer there to control me, I started rebelling. By the time I was thirteen, I was always hanging with friends, drinking, and experimenting with drugs.

First it was marijuana and then it was whiskey. Forget about beer. I hated the taste, and it took too long to get a buzz. But Scotch, now that was a different story. I loved the way it slid down my throat, delivering instant relief from the pain.

Pretty soon I got caught for breaking and entering. By then I was just following the crowd, looking for excitement and a little money to put in my pocket. When my mom walked into the police station and saw me with my hands and feet cuffed to a chair, the look on her face broke my heart. But it didn't convince me to stop. Instead I decided to become a little slicker. I had to find ways to hide what I was doing so I wouldn't hurt her anymore.

On my fourteenth birthday I hit the clubs for the first time. Nobody asked my friends or me for ID. They didn't bother back then. I started going to other clubs—Studio 54, the Inferno, the Palladium. I loved them all. And why not? There was so much sex, drugs, and alcohol—everything I needed for a good time.

I was hanging with friends, drinking, and experimenting with drugs.

By then I was smoking forty to fifty joints a day and freebasing cocaine. I liked tripping on acid and doing Tuinals, Seconals, Black Beauties. You name it. I took them all.

My dad had always told me I was stupid. Now my family started saying I was crazy. So now I was stupid *and* crazy— crazy stupid. *Okay, if that's what they think, that's what I'll be.* I just got worse.

"Alex, there's death in your eyes," they would say. "It looks like you don't even care."

And I didn't.

One day an older friend, a guy who was always in and out of jail, schooled me in how to shake down a john. He took me to Pacific and Fourth, where there was a lot of sex for sale. He would make deals with the women, saying, "Look, this is what you're gonna do. Get into my car, and when the john comes, you're gonna leave the door open and get him into a compromising position. Then I'm gonna come along and throw you out like I'm ripping you off. I'll take his pants off, grab whatever he has, and take off. We can split the money." So this is what we did.

I had a .38-caliber pistol and would shove it in the guy's face. Though I was only a kid, something in the way I looked convinced the john I would pull the trigger if he challenged me.

Meanwhile I was still in school, still popular and not even close to flunking out. I had an awesome teacher who tried to get through to me. "Alex," he would say, "you're a smart kid. I know you're in a bad situation, but you can get out of it." But I didn't want out of it.

Before long I started selling drugs on my own. It was so easy to make money, thousands of dollars a week. And it was even easier to spend it. My friends and I would drop a ton of money in bars and clubs. I don't know how much cash I took in over the course of a year, but by then I could have bought a couple of brownstones and a couple of cars with the money I spent on drugs.

I would stay up for two, three, four days straight without a wink of sleep. Because I was always high or drunk, I got into twelve car accidents. Two times I went through the windshield. I've been beaten with bats and attacked with knives. I've been shot at several times. Drug deals would go bad, or someone would think you were moving in on their territory, or guys would jump you to rip you off. I don't know how I survived any of it, especially that time on the Belt Parkway.

One time I was beating a guy with a bat, just hammering him. Though everyone else had fled, I noticed a man standing nearby, watching me. Who did he think he was? Before I could take the bat to him, he said, "How would you like a job? I need a guy like you." Then he offered me a big paycheck to become his point man. After that I acted as his go-to guy, picking up money from all his drug deals.

—

Would I end up killing someone, or getting killed?

—

On the outside I looked like somebody who didn't care about anything, scared of nothing and no one. But the truth is, I was terrified of how far I might go. Would I end up killing someone, or getting killed? Inside, I wasn't that tough. I was just trying to fit in, to prove things to people. I remember guys crying when I told them I was going to shoot them. They would have laughed in my face had they known how scared I really was.

After that episode on the Belt Parkway, I started thinking about my life. I was twenty-seven and already feeling old.

When you live like that, you know you aren't going to last long. I'd already lost at least twenty people who were important to me, mostly from drug violence. Before I died, I wanted to fall in love, get married, and become a dad. I really wanted children. Not long after that I met a nice girl and we got married.

My wife and I moved into a loft apartment with a huge living room. It was great for parties. I'd have ten guys in there playing congas. Right in the middle of everything would be a plate full of cocaine and marijuana. Our house quickly became party central.

Even while I was dealing, I always worked a regular job, often in construction. My fellow employees became part of my drug network, because everybody wanted drugs. On Thursday nights we would start partying. Knowing they were getting paid on Friday, people would ask me for credit. By Sunday they owed me again.

When my wife became pregnant, I was elated. But six months later she lost the baby. Then she got pregnant again. After several more months, she miscarried again. By then I was pretty sure I knew what the problem was. It was me! I was the problem. I didn't deserve to be a dad. I was a bad guy who'd done a lot of terrible things. Why should I be happy? Why should I be blessed with a child? I was sure my wife could have had a kid if she'd married someone else.

Then she became pregnant a third time. At first everything went well. But one day we ended up in the emergency room. While I was in the waiting room, worrying about my wife and baby, I did something I'd never done before, not even when I was hiding from somebody who was trying to kill me. I had always figured I could handle things on my own—but I couldn't handle this. So with my head in my hands, I prayed, not quietly in a whisper or silently in my heart, but out loud. "God, I don't know how to talk to you," I said. "I don't even know who I'm talking to. I don't know how to ask for anything. But if there is ever a time you want to make yourself real to me, this is the time. Please let my kid live. I promise to be a good dad. I'll take care of my wife. If you protect the baby, I'll serve you. I'll do whatever you want."

Then a wiseguy who was sitting nearby piped up: "Oh, he can't hear you," he said, like he was trying to be funny. Instead of taking a chair to his head like I wanted to, I walked over and stared at him. Then he walked away.

Five minutes later the nurse came in. "Mr. Colon," she said, "your wife is going to be okay. Everything is going to be fine."

I was so happy. I wanted to celebrate. Incredibly, after what I had just said to God, my first thought was, *I gotta roll me up a big fat cigarette of marijuana with a lot of cocaine in it!*

—

If there is ever a time you want to make yourself real to me, this is the time. Please let my kid live.

—

But as my wife and I walked through the double doors of the hospital, I saw two chrome garbage cans, one on either side of the doorway. I reached into my pockets and dropped a bag of cocaine in one can and a bag of weed in the other. Then I told my wife I would never touch drugs again.

This wasn't the first time I tried to quit. But I could never go for more than five minutes. I had been high every day for the last seventeen years, and I didn't have the strength to stop. No wonder my wife just shrugged when I told her I was quitting.

It wasn't easy for me that night. I wanted to sneak back to the hospital and retrieve those two bags of drugs. I knew I could manage it without waking my wife. But something prevented me. *Don't do it. Don't do it.* I kept hearing the words in my head.

Two weeks later, I was still clean. But after carrying the baby for six and a half months, my wife miscarried. I was so angry. "We had a deal," I told God. "I did my part. You didn't do yours." Surprisingly, I still had a measure of peace, enough to know I didn't want to go back to the way I had been living.

As I struggled with my hurt and disappointment, I felt like God was saying, *Alex, you stopped doing drugs for yourself, not for me. You knew you needed to get clean. Now you can see what you're capable of when I help you.*

So I did my best to comfort my wife. I told her we would find a way through this. Instead of being angry all the time, I tried to find solutions, to make things better for both of us. Shortly after that I landed a new job with great money. It was as if God was telling me I didn't have to sell drugs anymore, didn't need to keep living the way I had been.

Even though drugs and alcohol had always had such a powerful grip on me, God just lifted me up and gave me the strength to quit. I tell people I went through a one-step program, not a twelve-step program. After that day in the waiting room, I never took drugs or drank alcohol again.

How did I even know enough to call on God? People in my family always said they were Catholic. But they would only go to church on Easter. I had one aunt who was the real deal. She really loved God and it showed, and this aunt never gave up on me.

I remember one relative slamming the door in my face because she didn't want anything to do with me, didn't want her kids hanging around with me. I felt so small, so worthless, like a piece of garbage. But I never felt like that when I was with this aunt. She was always so kind and welcoming. Through all those hard years, she encouraged me and planted seeds in my life. Now they were starting to bear fruit.

One day I heard about a guy I knew named Angel. He'd been on crack and all kinds of crazy stuff. Somebody told me he was on fire for God. I couldn't believe it. But they invited me to a prayer meeting he attended. When I saw him I was shocked by how much he had changed. Though I had never liked him before, the two of us became best friends. And he became a mentor to me.

During the prayer meeting that night, I heard the pastor say something that went straight to my heart. Though there were thousands of people in the meeting, I felt like God was talking just to me. "You may not have had an earthly father," the pastor said, "someone who was good to you, someone who was kind to you, someone who was an example to you— but you have a heavenly Father who will never leave you, who will never forsake you, who will always be there for you." I lost it when I heard that.

I went home and told my wife what had happened. I had already asked God's forgiveness for so many things. He was changing me, making me into a different man. But instead of being happy about it, she said, "I really don't like the man you've become. I want the old Alex back, and I'm telling you that if you don't straighten out, I'm going to walk out."

Our house had always been party central. But no longer. I had rounded up all the liquor bottles we had—about three hundred—and tossed them out. "Listen," I would tell my friends. "You guys can come over and hang out, but you're not going to talk vulgar. You're not going to be smoking and drinking and taking drugs." I even told my wife she had to stop smoking cigarettes in the house. No wonder she was having a hard time adjusting to the new Alex.

Pretty soon nobody was stopping by. Whenever I tried to visit old friends, it was like Moses parting the Red Sea—half of them would go this way; the other half would go that way. Nobody wanted anything to do with me.

One day when I came home from work, I saw somebody moving furniture into a big truck. *Who's moving out?* I wondered. *Wait a minute! That looks a lot like my furniture.* Then I realized my wife was leaving me, and she was taking everything with her.

At one point she had given me an ultimatum: "Alex, we can't go on like this. You have to choose. It's either me or Jesus.

"Listen," I told her, "I'm not going to choose between either of you. I love you. I love the Lord. I am not going to choose. Do what you have to do. If you think you have to leave, take whatever you want." So she left and took everything.

Now my huge apartment was completely empty. I sat down on the floor of what had become one big echo chamber and wept. After a while I decided a drive might calm me down. Maybe if I drove around and listened to some music I could get my head together. But when I went downstairs to the garage, I couldn't find the car. Someone had stolen it!

By then I was really stressed out. I argued with God. *Why did you let this happen to me? I used to have everything. I had my family, my wife. Now I have nothing.* I couldn't imagine things getting any worse. But they did.

As soon as I walked upstairs to the apartment, my stomach started cramping up. I went to the bathroom, and I saw blood in the toilet—lots of it. I called 911. Medics arrived and carried me down four flights of stairs and into an ambulance. Then they drove me to a hospital where one of my sisters worked. As soon as a patient came in, boom, everything would come up on her screen. She saw my name. "Alex Colon."

Even though she wasn't speaking to me at the time, she ran through the hospital and found me. "I'm here," she said. "What happened? Are you okay?" Then she told the rest of my family, and they all came running.

Every member of my family had thought I was crazy, first for doing so many bad things and then for going to church and always talking about God. They blamed me for my wife's unhappiness, saying she was too good for me. She had a great job; she was college-educated. I was just a guy from the streets. Why did I keep pulling her down?

But as soon as they heard I was ill, everything changed. There were no more accusations; there was no more blame. Only love and concern. Though I had lost my wife, God gave me back the rest of my family. A lot of friends came back too. Though we were never as close again, they respected me. They knew I would be there for them no matter what.

Fortunately I made a complete recovery.

Eventually even my dad and I reconciled. Though he never knew half the things I had done, I started telling him so that he could understand how God had rescued me. I also let him know that I had forgiven him for not being a good father and for always putting himself first. Though he tried not to show it, I could tell my words were having an impact.

"Dad, whenever somebody dies," I told him, "people try to comfort each other. They say, 'He went to a better place.' But that's the biggest lie of the devil. Not everyone goes to a better place. You need Christ in your life. He loves you and will forgive you for everything if you will just ask him."

What a contrast with how I had felt as a kid. I remember thinking about how I could murder this man. *If he was drunk enough, could I push him through that window, or could he fall on a nice big knife?* I was a kid. I shouldn't have been thinking about such things, but he was hurting my mom, giving her black eyes. But now I really cared about him.

—

That's the biggest lie of the devil. Not everyone goes to a better place.

—

Within about a year and a half, my dad died. Though I didn't get to the hospital in time, my sisters told me what had happened. He had always been so hard-boiled, so cold. Nothing could make him cry. Even if a hammer slammed into his hand, he wouldn't have shed a tear. But he cried for an hour right before he died. He asked my mother to forgive him. He asked my sisters to forgive him. He asked my brother to forgive him. He said he was sorry for being such a terrible husband and father. He went right down the line, and then he lifted up his hands and asked God to forgive him.

If I hadn't been straight with him, I don't think any of it

would have happened. But because Jesus loved my dad, he gave me the strength to talk to him.

My beautiful little girl

Pretty soon my friend Angel got married. I met his wife's best friend, and the two of us hit it off. But I wasn't ready to get married again, not yet. I told her about all the terrible things I had done. She heard everything. Four years later we married, and two years after that we had a beautiful little girl. I was finally able to be the dad I always longed to be.

God has done so much for me. He rescued me when I was in despair. He cleaned me up and restored my life. He blessed me with a wonderful family and great relationships. He gave me so much hope. The reason Jesus died on the cross was for people like me. It was for people who have no hope. There's no limit to his strength, to his power, to his love, to his compassion. He's there with his arms open wide, just waiting for us to come home.

TONI'S STORY

_____

DR. TONI GINÉS-RIVERA IS THE DIRECTOR OF THE ALLIANCE GRADUATE SCHOOL OF COUNSELING AT NYACK COLLEGE IN NEW YORK CITY. BECAUSE OF THE SIGNIFI-CANT HEADWINDS SHE FACED IN THE EARLY YEARS OF HER LIFE, NO ONE WOULD HAVE VOTED HER THE GIRL MOST LIKELY TO SUCCEED. NOR WOULD THEY HAVE PREDICTED THE PATH HER HEALING WOULD TAKE.

I AM LYING IN MY HOSPITAL BED after giving birth. No one is with me except the social worker assigned to my case. I remember thinking how kind and gentle she is, like you would want your mother to be. She asks how I'm feeling, as though she really cares about me and my baby.

She doesn't pressure me by saying things like, "Who's the father, Toni?" or "If you want help, you've got to tell us what happened."

My mother asks these questions all the time, but I stonewall. "I don't know," I tell her.

—

No matter who questions me, the answer is always the same: *I don't know*.

—

"What do you mean you don't know? What's his name?" She's determined to pry the secret out of me.

"I forget," I say.

No matter who questions me, the answer is always the same: *I don't know . . . I don't know . . . I don't know.*

But now the social worker is asking me a question that I am trying to answer. "What would you like to name him, Toni?"

I'm at a loss for what to say. My baby needs a name, but I've never thought about what I will call him. For the last several months I have been living in the moment, focused only on surviving. I've had no energy to consider the things that preoccupy most pregnant women. There is no list of baby names for me to ponder.

"Toni, you just had a boy," she repeats quietly. "What would you like to name him?" Then she smiles at me, like I have done something amazing by giving birth to my nine-pound baby.

Suddenly I hear an announcement over the intercom: "Dr. Ruben, Dr. Ruben, please come to conference room four in the east wing."

Turning to the social worker, I say, "What a beautiful name! Am I allowed to give my son that name? It's so beautiful."

Assuring me that I can name my baby whatever I want to, she writes his name on a piece of paper, spelling it out for me, *R-u-b-e-n.*

After she leaves, with my son cradled in my arms, I say it aloud several times. "Ruben, my little Ruben." And the name on my lips tastes like love.

———

I was only a young girl myself, just barely fifteen, when Ruben came into the world. Years later I ran across an old photo. It was a picture of me as an eleven-month-old child. As I stared at the photo, I began to cry, because it was impossible to ignore the fear in that child's eyes, as though she could already see what was coming.

Fear always comes from somewhere. When I was a little girl, it came from having an alcoholic father and a seventeen-year-old mother who weighed only ninety-nine pounds but could swear like a sailor. It came from never being kissed or hugged or told I was loved or that I mattered. It came from attempting to be a "little mother" to my four younger siblings, who were born in rapid succession. It came from a home that was chaos all the time.

While Mom was overwhelmed with the demands of caring for five children, my dad had troubles of his own that were made far worse by his drinking. As a child living in Puerto Rico, he'd been given to neighbors to be raised. Since his mother still lived in the neighborhood while he was growing up, he relived this rejection every time he saw her.

By then my family was living in California, but things weren't going well. I was five years old when my dad's half brother moved in after being discharged from the army. Since he was our uncle, we called him Tió. Unlike Dad, my uncle wasn't drunk all the time, which was enough to make him look like a knight in shining armor to my mom.

—

Unlike Dad, my uncle wasn't drunk all the time, which was enough to make him look like a knight in shining armor to my mom.

—

Since Dad worked nights, it didn't take long for my mom and Tió to begin an affair. As they grew closer, I remember seeing and hearing things no child should witness. Their relationship confused me and made me wonder how my dad fit in. Even when he was home, he was pretty much not there. He just tuned out and gave my uncle free reign.

So Tió was a game changer. When my mother allowed herself to be conquered by him, she had no idea that her decision would damage the family in ways that would haunt us for years.

Shortly before my tenth birthday, my parents decided to move us all to New York. Dad went first with a couple of his brothers. He was supposed to get a job and find a place for us to live. But my father didn't land a job, and we had no place to live. So when my mom and Tió arrived, we stayed with an aunt. Because my mom wouldn't permit my dad to move in without a job, he just drifted away. Meanwhile, Tió found his own place to live.

Even though he didn't live with us, Tió was always there, acting like a stand-in husband and father. When I was ten, he began shifting his attention to me. I never knew why. Perhaps by then my mother had come to her senses and was trying to get out from under his thumb. But she couldn't get rid of him.

Meanwhile my uncle began giving me small gifts and telling me how much he loved me. One day he sat me on his lap at a family gathering. I was so uncomfortable that I tried pulling away, but he held me tight and began telling me how special I was. The party was packed with people, but there was so much going on that nobody noticed anything. "Don't worry, I love you," he whispered. "You're like my daughter. I would never hurt you, Ontonette," as he called me.

Some part of me needed to hear what Tió was saying: that I was cherished, that I was important, that I was loved. I was like a small plant that had managed to sprout in a cracked, dry patch of earth. Now, finally, someone was watering that little plant so it could flourish. Of course it was all a lie, but it was one I wanted to believe. It was wonderful to think that somebody could love me as his own daughter.

—

Some part of me needed to hear what Tió was saying: that I was cherished, that I was important, that I was loved.

—

It wasn't long before he began to abuse me sexually. He was forty-five and I was ten.

By then I wasn't the only one in the house who was being abused. Whenever my brothers didn't do exactly as Tió said, he would beat them.

As the eldest of five children, I was like a little mother to my sister and brothers, taking care of them whenever Mom was too tired or depressed to deal with things. When she was out or feeling depressed, I would boil the eggs or the hot dogs to feed us. It didn't matter if Tió was there. He never tried to help.

My uncle had begun by making me feel special. Though part of me loved the extra attention, I felt guilty about how he was treating my siblings. But it wasn't long until any feeling of being chosen or specially selected evaporated. I had been reduced to one of his possessions, something Tió owned and could use and abuse as he pleased. Saturdays were always the worst day of the week for me because my mother would leave the house to attend cosmetology school and put me in charge.

"Don't leave! Please take me with you," I would beg her. But the answer was always the same. She needed me to stay home and take care of the rest of the family.

As soon as she left, Tió would arrive. It was part of the routine, the way he did business. Ordering my sister and brothers outside to play on the street, he would take me into the bedroom and rape me. While he was molesting me, I wasn't screaming or crying. Instead I was worrying about my little sister. She was only four years old and playing on the streets of Brooklyn with no one to watch her. Tió's abuse continued for the next five years. Whenever Mom was out, he would arrive. While she was gone, he did whatever he wanted.

Not long after my fourteenth birthday, his attitude toward me shifted. Now he was becoming violent, beating me and threatening to throw me down the stairs. I remember hanging on to the banister and begging for my life. He made me swallow pills and various concoctions and forced me to wear a tight corset girdle that cut painfully into my abdomen.

—

Because I didn't even know I was pregnant, it took me a long time to figure out what Tió was trying to do.

—

No one had ever taught me anything about my body or about what to expect when I reached puberty. I knew nothing about menstrual cycles or any of the changes I was undergoing. Because I didn't even know I was pregnant, it took me a long time to figure out what Tió was trying to do. This new level of abuse was intended to get rid of the baby, to erase the evidence of what he'd been doing to me.

When none of it worked, he took me to the local hospital. Because we shared a last name it wasn't hard for him to pose as my father. Though he tried to schedule an abortion, the doctor refused because the pregnancy was already in its third trimester.

On February 14, when I was seven months pregnant, Tió shoved a Valentine's Day card into my hands and ordered me to write this note: *Dear Mom, I'm letting you know I don't love you, and I'm running away. You're not a good mother. Don't look for me, because you're not going to find me.*

But it was all a big lie. Despite her failings, I loved my mom. In fact I'd always felt a lot of compassion for her. I would never have run away. But I couldn't summon the strength to fight back. So I wrote the message on the card and then signed it, tears streaming down my face.

Years later my youngest brother told me what he remembers about that day. Though he was supposed to stay in the living room with the other kids, he could hear me sobbing. Since we lived in a railroad-style apartment, he had to creep through the living room and the bedrooms to get near the kitchen. Even so he couldn't quite figure out what was happening. "I wanted to know what Tió was making you do," he told me, "and why you were crying so much. Then you just disappeared."

Tió had abducted me.

I was so terrified of my uncle that it was a relief when he dropped me off at a stranger's home—a very small apartment that belonged to a woman with a daughter who was about my age. Until then I had been good at keeping the secret, because Tió had always threatened to hurt me and my family if I said anything. But as often happens with teenagers, the woman's daughter and I quickly became friends, especially since we shared a bed. Eventually I told her everything, and she told her mother.

Soon my own mother was on the phone, crying hysterically. By then I'd been missing for two months. "Toni, where are you? I need to come get you! Why did you run away?" she kept pressing me, but I was too afraid to tell her what happened.

"Are you on drugs?"

"No," I replied.

Continuing to probe, she finally hit on it. "Are you pregnant?" When her question was met with silence, she said,

"You're pregnant, aren't you? Don't worry. We'll work through this. It's okay. I'm going to come get you."

But instead of picking me up, she called Tió, and he insisted on coming to get me. No doubt he had been playing the part of the concerned uncle the whole time I was away.

You can imagine our conversation as soon as I climbed into his car. Under no circumstances was I to tell anyone who the father of my baby was. I was instructed to say I didn't know.

After I returned home my mother's interrogations began. "Who is the father?"

I don't know.

"Where did you go with him?"

I don't know.

I would respond the same way to every question, breaking into hysterics as she continued to press me. How could I tell her the truth when my uncle was always there, listening to every word?

By then I was nine months pregnant. I hadn't seen an OB/ GYN or taken even one vitamin during the entire pregnancy. I had no idea what was involved in giving birth. When my mother finally took me to the doctor, he spoke of the importance of preparing me for the delivery, especially since I was going to have a big baby. But what did that mean? I didn't even realize it took nine months for a pregnancy to reach term, and I had no clue about the significance of having a big baby. I was in shock and frightened about everything that was happening to me.

—

**How could I tell her the truth
when my uncle was always there,
listening to every word?**

—

Though there were so many things I didn't understand, one thing was clear. As soon as I realized a baby was growing inside me, I made a choice to love him. Though I didn't know how to pray or who to pray to, I remember saying, "Please let me keep this baby. It's mine. This is mine. This is all that belongs to me in the world." Somehow the thought that I was going to have a baby strengthened my desire to live.

After Ruben was born, Tió bought a house and then moved the entire family into it. We lived on the top two floors while he had an apartment on the first floor. To deflect attention from me, my mother told everyone in our new neighborhood that Ruben was her baby. So it was no surprise that as soon as he could talk he began calling her Mommy and me Toni. Determined to teach him who I really was, I would take him aside and say, "No, no. I am Mommy. Call me Mommy." I didn't care what other people thought. If anyone asked why he was calling me "Mommy," I planned to respond with the answer I always gave—*I don't know.*

When I was sixteen, I returned to school. Like most teenagers, I began to want more control over my life. For the first time, I realized the extent to which Tió had been forcibly controlling me. Though he was no longer molesting me, he was still a one-man Gestapo, watching my every move, listening to everything I said, trying to control and isolate me. This middle-aged man was getting on my last nerve, cramping my style big time.

One day he came to pick me up after school. I was talking to a couple of friends and he kept beeping the horn, trying to hurry me up. I decided to ignore him, even though I knew I would pay a price for doing so. When I finally got in the car, he was in a rage. "Who do you think you are? Don't you ever ignore me again," he shouted, punching at me. "I will kill you if you do."

As soon as we got home, he dragged me into his apartment, slapping me, pulling my hair, and punching me in the face. Though I was used to being beaten, this time was different. Now all the rage and hatred I felt for him erupted, making its way from my heart to my mouth. Defying him, I fought back. But he was stronger than I was and threw me to the floor. I screamed as he began beating me, pummeling me with clenched fists like I was another man.

Assuming we were alone in the house that day, Tió must have been shocked when my mother came running. "What's going on?" she yelled.

"This girl is gonna learn some respect!" he roared.

While Tió was distracted, I leapt up from the floor. Blood was streaming down my face and onto my clothes. Even though my nose was broken, I was determined not to cry. There was no way I was going to give him the satisfaction.

I remember looking at my mother as I headed out the door. When I saw the hopeless, desolate look on her face, I knew that she could no longer hide the truth from herself. "You know what's going on here. And if you *really* want to know, ask him!" I said, walking out the door.

That day Tió told my mother that he was Ruben's father. I don't know what happened after that, but I remember the screaming. Later that night she snuck into his apartment, grabbed his gun, and put it to his head while he was sleeping. Then she chased him out of the house and up the street.

Of all the difficulties in my mother's life, this was the worst. For the first time, she had to face the fact that her daughter was being abused by a man she had allowed to take control of her life and mine.

My Aunt Elsie, the only Christian in our family, was forever inviting Mom to church, but she never went. She had no interest. But after that showdown with Tió, my aunt invited her to her house, explaining that she was asking a few friends to gather for prayer. When my mother went that night, she surrendered her life to Christ.

When Jesus came in, he changed everything for us. My mother was so different that it almost seemed as if God had done surgery on her. Suddenly she had a backbone. She wasn't depressed anymore but was full of energy and certainty. There was a new peace about her. Years earlier, when she had first given in to Tió and then allowed him to take over our lives, it had nearly destroyed our family. But now her complete surrender to Christ lifted everyone up.

Shortly after that we moved out of Tió's house and into our own apartment.

At first we attended the little storefront church that my aunt went to. But I felt that everyone there was judging me for being a teenage mom. Though I had only a little bit of faith at the time, I used it to tell God that I didn't like going to that church. "Please," I prayed, "will you get us another one?"

A few days later, I was on a bus packed with people. There was a tiny black woman standing beside me. I remember watching her purse swinging back and forth on her arm as the bus lurched through traffic. Catching my eye, she spoke to me, "You're looking for a church, aren't you?" When I said that yes I was looking for a church, she pulled out a small piece of paper with an address on it—543 Atlantic Avenue. "Go there," she told me. "You're going to love it."

I had no idea how she had read my heart; I only knew that I had to visit that church. "Can we go, can we go?" I kept asking my mom.

The next Sunday we showed up at the church on Atlantic Avenue. The young pastor and his wife made us feel so welcome that we kept coming back. There were no accusations and no questions. No feeling that everyone was looking down on me. The pastor never brought me into his office and said, "Ok, Toni, I need to know. Where does that little boy come from? Who's the father? Are you getting any money from him? Who's supporting the two of you?" There was nothing like that.

Belonging to that church was like joining a wonderful family, having a new start in life. I saw something in that pastor that helped me realize for the first time what it would be like to have a father who was kind and protective. I began to realize that's who God is.

After a while, I met someone and fell in love. Though I was only seventeen at the time, I assured Benjie I was eighteen and old enough to date him. Three years later we married. We were so happy together. Getting married was a huge surprise for me. Because of my past I had felt irretrievably damaged, as though no one would ever want me after what had happened. But Benjie loved me unconditionally.

By now I was living a beautiful story. We were in church. I was in the choir. I had a wonderful husband who was also a great father to my child. On the outside things couldn't have been better. I was bubbly and cheerful most of the time. But on the inside trouble was brewing.

Instead of telling Benjie the story of my childhood, I told him I had made a youthful mistake with a boyfriend who was no longer in the picture. Though it made me look bad, there was no way I was going to tell him the truth—that my uncle had impregnated me and that he was Ruben's father. I wanted no more ugliness, no more unhappiness. I wanted to leave the past behind as though it had never happened.

I did such a great job burying my secret that I began to believe that Benjie was Ruben's birth father. When our daughter Aimee was born it seemed as though another wonderful chapter had opened in our lives. But leaning into a "happily ever after story" that I had made up in my head wouldn't work forever.

Though I knew the Lord at that time, my faith wasn't very strong. Looking back I understand that it's impossible to grow deep roots if your life is planted in falsehoods. Instead of opening up I had closed up tightly, hiding my shame and pretending to be a woman with no concerns about the past because she was so happy in the present.

Of course I didn't do all of this consciously. It was just so hard to face my shame head-on. But unacknowledged pain has a way of festering until it finally erupts. And after eight years of marriage, mine did. It happened in the middle of the night.

—

Everything I had tried to bury was coming up, and I didn't know what to do about it.

—

Unable to sleep, I stared at the framed portraits of my two children on the bedroom wall. I remember looking at Aimee and then at Ruben and then back at Aimee. When I looked at Ruben a second time, something shifted inside me. I began to feel sick as the truth about my past surfaced and memories started flooding my mind. Everything I had tried to bury was coming up, and I didn't know what to do about it.

The more I remembered my childhood trauma, the worse I felt. For a long time I thought about killing myself. I was twenty-eight years old and no longer wanted to live.

Instead of taking my life suddenly, I took it gradually. When I was thirty I gave birth to a baby we named Benjamin Jacob. By then Benjie and I had also adopted two of my nieces. As I slipped deeper into my own dark world, I stopped coping. Even though I never moved out of the house, I managed to abandon my husband and all five children.

I did it by walking out on them night after night. Pretty soon I had a new set of friends, people who only wanted to party. By then there was so much anger and rage in me that I hated everyone except the people who shared my love of drugs and drinking.

My husband had no idea what was happening because I had never told him about Tió. When you keep brushing the past off like it's no big deal, pretty soon people stop asking about it. Because of how I was acting, he began to believe that I had never really loved him. Maybe I had only married him in order to provide a father for Ruben. That started a trajectory of rejection that created even more chaos in our lives.

One night, high and drunk, I told my new posse the real story of what had happened to me as a child. Instead of listening sympathetically and advising me to get the help I needed, they only fueled my rage, saying it was time somebody took that guy out. Together my drug buddies and I devised a plan to find Tió and kill him—but we never caught up with him and I never saw him again. Years later I understood that it was God's love and protection that kept me from finding my uncle. Who knows what would have happened had we tracked him down?

No matter how many drugs I took or how much alcohol I consumed, I couldn't keep misery at bay. In fact my reactions were making it worse. Once I had been an innocent victim whose life had been devastated by the sins of the adults around her. Now I was an adult who was choosing to make her own bad decisions.

—

Once I had been an innocent victim
whose life had been devastated by
the sins of the adults around her.
Now I was an adult who was choosing
to make her own bad decisions.

—

Finally, in the midst of my desperation, I cried out to God. *Get me out of this mess!* I pleaded. *You've got to get me out. I don't care what it takes. Even if it means exposing my sin, please God rescue me!*

And God did. He came in and saved me in the deepest way possible. He forgave me, healed me, and restored me to my husband and children. When I finally went back to church after being gone for four years, no one scolded me. No one lectured me. No one turned their back on me. Instead they welcomed me back with so much love.

My husband was incredibly forgiving and loving toward me as well. Years after we reconciled, I asked him how he got through that awful time. Why hadn't he left me when he knew I'd abandoned our children and been unfaithful to him? How was he able to treat his troubled, broken wife with so much kindness?

"Toni," he said, "God gave me the book of Hosea in the Bible—you know, the one about the prophet who married this woman who kept turning her back on him? God told me to love you like Hosea loved his unfaithful wife because you were the wife of my youth. He got me through it all."

Indeed, God has brought us both through. My journey of healing has not been easy. It's taken a lot of hard work and time. I've had to face the pain and ugliness of my past head-on. But doing that in God's presence has not destroyed me. Instead it's brought me joy and freedom. It's also enabled me to help others.

When I was still a teenager, I had to drop out of school to help support my family. That meant no high school diploma. But I decided to get my GED at the age of thirty-five. Then one of my teachers suggested I would make a good school psychologist. With his encouragement I went on to college and completed a bachelor of arts in psychology. After that I received a master's degree from Fordham University in New York. Finally I received my PhD in counseling psychology. Since then I've had the chance to come alongside others who have suffered abuse and need someone to help them through the healing process.

Incredibly, I harbor no hatred for Tió. Forgiving him took time. It was a process, but one that God greatly blessed. I realize that what was meant for evil has been turned around for good. My beautiful son, Ruben, and my ability to help others who have suffered from abuse have both been gifts from God.

But the story doesn't end there. One day I received a surprising phone call from a cousin. The caller identified himself as Tió's son. He had just learned about what his father had done to me when I was a child and was calling to express his sorrow. As we talked I learned that Tió had recently passed away. Sensing that my cousin was the one in need of consolation, I told him that I had forgiven his father long ago.

Then he told me that he and his sister had spent years sharing the gospel with their father, though he had always been resistant. But on his deathbed Tió had repeated the sinner's prayer with his son, repenting of his sin and affirming his belief in Christ and his desire to entrust his life to him. I was glad to hear that my uncle had a chance to depart the world with a sense of peace.

I've always wondered whether my mother suspected what was happening long before the truth burst into the open. I will never know because we never resolved that issue before her untimely death. I do know that God has given me a lot of compassion for her. And I'm grateful that she finally stood up for me.

In some ways my babies helped save my life. They gave me a reason to live. Ruben was a ray of light in the midst of so much darkness, and Aimee was the little girl I'd always dreamed of having.

Though Benjamin was named after his father, it didn't occur to me until a few years after his birth that God was speaking to me through both of my sons' names. Perhaps you remember the story in the Bible of Jacob and his twelve sons. Ruben is the name of the first of his sons and Benjamin is the name of his last. When I named my sons, I hadn't heard about Jacob's story. I knew nothing of his struggles and how God helped him. Reading about his life made me realize that my own sons have been like bookends to my story, framing my life. Though Benjamin was born during my years of struggle, through his birth I found a reason to live once again.

Sadly he passed away three years ago from a rare blood disorder. Of everything I have suffered during the course of my life, this has been the worst by far. To lose him—a young man who was always so kind and loving, who was always a peacemaker—felt unbearable. And yet with God's help I have been able to bear even this pain. As I consider the future, I know that every day I need to lean on God, to be dependent on him as I take each new step. There is no other way and no turning back for me.

I've also come to realize that no life is easy. Because of what happened to me, I understand that there are two plans for every life. There's God's plan and Satan's plan. Satan will do everything in his power to make his plan for your life come true. The Bible counsels us to "be alert and of sober mind." It tells us that our "enemy the devil prowls around like a roaring lion looking for someone to devour" (I Peter 5:8). He will take every opportunity to destroy us.

With my son Ruben

But if you stretch out your hand and put it into God's hand, the plan that he's had for you since the beginning of time—the plan that only you can live out—will come into being and you will know joy and freedom. No matter how painful your story has been, or how much shame you might be hiding from yourself and others, God is strong and loving enough to deal with it. He's also creative enough to use everything—even the worst things—to accomplish his good purposes. If you let him, he will turn your life into a story that you will cherish, just as my son Ruben and I cherish ours today. We call it not "my story" but "our story" because of how God has blessed us both despite the difficult way in which Ruben was conceived and came into the world. The only question you have to answer right now is this: Who will you trust with the life you've been given? What kind of story will be yours?

THE RESCUER

_____

I hope you have enjoyed reading the stories of my seven friends as much as I have enjoyed telling them. As unique as each story is, there is a single thread that holds them all together. As each person's life spiraled downward, something unexpected happened. Someone heard their cries for help and rescued them.

But who is that someone, that rescuer who was able to transform broken, hopeless lives into something whole and strong and good? Each of my friends will tell you who that person is. If it weren't for Jesus, they will say, they would either be dead or trapped forever in a life of pain and darkness.

You probably know that Jesus was a Jewish rabbi who lived in a backwater region of the Roman Empire. A popular preacher, his teaching was considered so incendiary and subversive by the religious elites of his day that they couldn't tolerate him for even three years—the length of his public ministry. Jealous of his influence, they plotted to kill him.

When Jesus was nailed to a Roman cross, even his closest followers thought that his life had ended in complete failure. No one realized that by accepting the punishment for our sins he was performing the most loving, heroic, and powerful act in the history of the world. Through his willing sacrifice, he was opening up a way for sinful human beings to return to God.

After his resurrection, as one person after another—even some of the elites who had earlier opposed him—gave their lives to Jesus and became transformed by his love, the world as we know it began to change.

Two thousand years later, Jesus is still in the business of changing lives as people cry out to him for help. Because Jesus, as God's Son, is both human and divine, he is the only being in the universe capable of bridging the vast abyss between sinful humans and a holy God.

At the heart of every life, including yours and mine, is a choice. Will we keep doing things our way, calling all the shots and living as though we are in control, or will we cry out to Jesus, asking him to come into our lives and show us the way to live?

Because Jesus desires our love, he will never force us to come to him. He knows that love is only love if it is freely given. So he invites us into an intimate relationship with himself and then leaves the choice to us. We can either refuse that relationship or accept it.

If you decide to accept it and if you want to make a fresh start in your life, begin by asking Jesus to forgive the sins you've committed in the past. Make no excuses or rationalizations. The reason he died on the cross was to provide pardon for you and me. Then trust him to handle the present and the future— today and tomorrow and the day after that.

Jesus is the only one who can give you a fresh start, the only one who can help you begin again. No matter what you've done or what's been done to you, he can give you a new heart and a new mind and the kind of peace and joy that doesn't fluctuate with circumstances. The only thing he cannot do is fail to rescue you when you commit your life to him.

If you're tired of living life your way, and if you want to know God more deeply, join me in this prayer:

God, I thank you for creating me in your image. Even when I was far away from you, you didn't give up on me. Instead you made it possible for me to come back to you by sending your Son, Jesus Christ, who took the punishment I deserved by dying on the cross and who was then raised from the dead. I ask you to forgive all my sins and teach me how to live. I renounce Satan and all his ways and ask you to break his power in my life. I want nothing to do with him. Instead I want to surrender my life to Jesus Christ, whom I accept as my Lord and Savior. Please fill me with your Holy Spirit and give me the faith I need to follow wherever you lead. Amen.

WHERE TO GO FROM HERE

If you have surrendered your life to Jesus, you can be sure that God and his angels are celebrating right now. By virtue of saying yes to his invitation, you have become his adopted son or daughter, a beloved child who is part of his family. Because your sins have been washed away, he sees them no more. You have begun to live a new life.

Now that you have joined God's family, what's next? By entering into a relationship with Jesus and your heavenly Father, you've been transferred from the kingdom of darkness to the kingdom of light. Instead of being God's enemy, you've now become his good friend.

Your new status brings tremendous blessings. Because of God's eternal love and his great faithfulness, you will live with him forever. Here on earth he will help you and equip you to live a life of faithfulness, which will bring you tremendous peace and joy.

Though God may decide to heal you quickly from the hurts you have suffered as a result of your sins and the sins that others have committed against you, more often that healing will come gradually. You will experience more and more freedom and healing as you begin to follow Jesus, who is the Great Physician.

Sometimes you will find yourself encountering obstacles. This can happen because part of you still wants to do things the way you used to, as though you, and not Jesus, are in charge of your life. When you stumble, simply get up and ask your Father's forgiveness. He will surely give it.

Belonging to Jesus is all about transformation. If you want to experience deep happiness, you have to begin by knowing why you were created. You need to know your purpose. The first chapter of the Bible tells us that "God created human beings in his own image. In the image of God he created them; male and female he created him." (Genesis 1:27 New Living Translation). That means that you and I and every person who has ever lived were created with the primary purpose of being filled up with God. We are to follow Jesus so closely and to know him so intimately that we become like him, reflecting his character. Shining with his presence and being filled up with his life will make us happy like nothing else can.

A primary way to grow closer to God is to read the Bible, which is his personal Word to us. In the Bible he communicates his heart. He tells us who he is and how we are to live. This is particularly true in the New Testament, which focuses on the life of Jesus and the early church. If you're not familiar with the Bible, start by purchasing a good translation, one that is written in today's English. Begin by reading the Gospel of John, and then continue to read the New Testament and the Psalms, which can be a great help in prayer.

Pay particular attention to the wonderful promises God has made to those who love him. Here are just a few that are worth reflecting on daily.

Do not be anxious about anything, but in every situation, by prayer and petition, with thanksgiving, present your requests to God. (Philippians 4:6)

If we confess our sins, he is faithful and just and will forgive us our sins and purify us from all unrighteousness. (I John I: 9)

Come to me, all you who are weary and burdened, and I will give you rest. Take my yoke upon you and learn from me, for I am gentle and humble in heart, and you will find rest for your souls. (Matthew II: 28–29)

"For I know the plans I have for you," declares the Lord, "plans to prosper you and not to harm you, plans to give you hope and a future." (Jeremiah 29:11)

For I am convinced that neither death nor life, neither angels nor demons, neither the present nor the future, nor any powers, neither height nor depth, nor anything else in all creation, will be able to separate us from the love of God that is in Christ Jesus our Lord. (Romans 8:38–39)

Let us then approach God's throne of grace with confidence, so that we may receive mercy and find grace to help us in our time of need. (Hebrews 4:16)

Remember that the one who has made these promises to you is faithful. He is your heavenly Father, who watches over you with his strong, protective love.

Because he is a good Father, he wants to stay close to you, to listen to you as you pray. Don't worry about the exact words you use—just pour out your heart to him. Don't be afraid to bring him your deepest troubles and your most pressing questions. Simply lift them up to him and trust that he will guide you. Wait patiently for him to act, to provide you with the grace and wisdom you need in every situation. Remember that you can have fellowship with God because you and he are no longer strangers but good friends. Nothing can separate you from his love.

As you spend time with him daily, remember to begin by praising him for who he is and thanking him for how he has worked in your life. By doing so, you will find your faith growing stronger and your love deepening.

In addition to reading the Bible and praying daily, it is vital that you find a good church home where you can connect with other believers. Though no church is perfect, ask God to help you find one that will help you grow. Look for a church in which the leaders and members express a living relationship with Jesus Christ, basing their lives on the truths of the Bible, and depending on God's grace to help them grow. It's important to meet at least weekly with other believers so that you can worship God, pray together, and hear God's Word proclaimed. We all need Christian friends who can support and encourage us when we need it most.

Having a living relationship with Jesus Christ will bring you tremendous joy. But you will still have struggles, some of which will arise because of spiritual opposition. Though Satan has always been your enemy, he hates you even more because you now belong to God. But you needn't be afraid of him. Jesus will protect you as you stay close to him, giving you everything you need. As Scripture says, "In all things God works for the good of those who love him" (Romans 8:28).

That means that even our difficulties will benefit us as long as we stay close to Jesus.

Like my friends Lawrence, Timiney, Rich, Robin, Kaitlin, Alex, and Toni, you will encounter challenges as you live this new life. But the joy and victory that belong to you because of your relationship with Jesus will far outweigh them.

As we close our time together, I want to invite you to imagine once again that all of us are sitting down in my living room. Now you know the stories of my friends and why they aren't afraid to tell them. As we thank God for everything he has done, let me leave you with this prayer of blessing, which was first prayed by the Apostle Paul for the early Christians.

I pray that out of his glorious riches, he [God] may strengthen you with power through his Spirit in your inner being, so that Christ may dwell in your hearts through faith. And I pray that you, being rooted and established in love, may have power, together with all the Lord's holy people, to grasp how wide and long and high and deep is the love of Christ, and to know this love that surpasses knowledge—that you may be filled to the measure of all the fullness of God. (Ephesians 3:16–19)

HOW TO WATCH
"THE RESCUE"

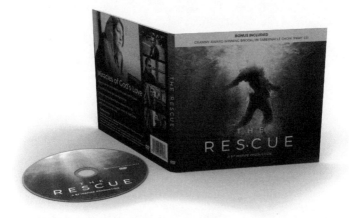

Five of the stories you have just read can
be viewed online. To watch the video for free,
visit *www.TheRescue.nyc/watch*

ALSO BY
JIM CYMBALA

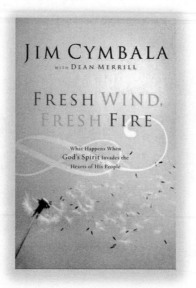

The compelling story of what happened to
The Brooklyn Tabernacle—a broken-down church in one
of America's toughest neighborhoods—points the way to
new spiritual vitality in the church and in your own life.

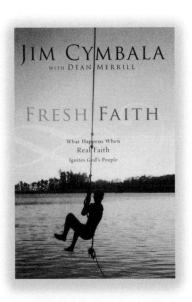

Faith is what stirs God to move miraculously
on our behalf. If you wonder if God has fallen
asleep at the wheel while you or your loved ones face
challenge after challenge, discover how faith that is not
"trying harder to believe" but that is real, simple, and
completely dependent on God, can change your life.